W9-BGD-491

LIBERATING
JESUS

Copyright © 2021 Leonard Jacobson

CONSCIOUS LIVING
PUBLICATIONS

Liberating Jesus

All rights reserved.
No part of this book may be reproduced
in any form or by any means whatsoever,
whether electronic or mechanical, including
photocopying and phonographic recording,
nor may it be stored in a retrieval system,
transmitted or otherwise copied for private
or public use without the prior written
consent of the author, except for the
inclusion of brief quotations for review.

Library of Congress Control Number: 2021904446

ISBN: 978-1-890580-12-4

First paperback printing June, 2021

Printed in the United States of America

10 9 8 7 6 5 4 3 2 1

Library of Congress Cataloging-in-Publication data

Jacobson, Leonard 1944-

For Mary,
my beloved wife who passed away in 2018.
Her tireless love and devotion supported me
through the whole process of writing
and performing Liberating Jesus.

And for Jim & Jane,
who stepped up and made themselves available
when I needed them the most. They have very generously
taken over the day to day running of the
Conscious Living Foundation,
a non-profit organization that
supports this teaching.

And for Sue,
whose love and generosity introduced and
supports the sharing of my teaching in China.

And for Neil & Petra,
whose loving and supportive friendship
has enabled me to continue with this teaching
long after I should have retired.

And for the many students and seekers of truth
who have participated in this teaching over
the past 40 years. It is your courage and honesty
that has allowed me to see deeply
into the human soul and witness
the magnificence within.

OTHER BOOKS
BY LEONARD JACOBSON

Words from Silence
Embracing the Present
Bridging Heaven & Earth
Journey into Now
In Search of the Light

CONSCIOUS LIVING
PUBLICATIONS

LIBERATING JESUS

Part 1
Awakenings

Part 2
The Script of the Play

Part 3
Questions & Answers

LEONARD JACOBSON

INTRODUCTION

This is a book about Jesus. Who was he really? What was his true mission upon this planet? What is the true meaning of his words? What happened during the crucifixion? What has happened to him since his death upon the cross? How is his teaching still relevant to the awakening of human consciousness? What would Jesus say if he returned today?

As a result of a series of awakening experiences which began in 1981, I received a flow of revelations that provided answers to these questions. How this came about is described in Part 1 of this book on 'Awakenings.'

But this is also a book about the awakening of human consciousness in a more general sense. I have been sharing my teaching on awakening since 1982. In those early days, not many people knew what was meant by awakening and not many people were interested. Humanity is functioning at a largely unconscious level which has caused so much suffering in our world. We cannot continue living in this way. We have reached a critical point in our existence. If we are to survive, we will have to change the way we live upon this planet. There will have to be an awakening of consciousness at a collective level.

What do I mean by awakening? What are we awakening from? What are we awakening to?

In the simplest terms, we are awakening from the past and future world of the mind into the world of the present moment. We are awakening from illusion into truth. We are awakening from the feeling of being separate to the experience of Oneness. We are awakening into the present moment and a state of consciousness which I call Presence. As we awaken into Presence, our lives will be transformed in a very positive way, but more importantly it will transform how we live upon this planet. It will change the way we relate to each other and to the natural environment.

Almost the whole of humanity is functioning at a very limited level of consciousness, which I call the world of the mind. It is a vast and complex field of dreams. It is a world of the remembered past and the imagined future. It is a world of never-ending thought. It is a world of idea, concept, opinion and belief. It is illusory in nature and it is based in separation. When you are in the mind, you are under the control of the ego. You live with fear, desire, judgment and all the limiting beliefs which formed within your mind in early childhood. You also live with all the repressed feelings that have accumulated within you over the years.

When you become present, you open into love, acceptance and compassion. You open into true power. You exist in the realization of Oneness. At the deeper levels of Presence, you just might experience the living Presence of God in all things present. At the deepest level of awakened Presence, you might also open into the experience of Heaven on Earth.

By way of introduction, I would like to share with you a little of my own journey, which led to the formation of my teaching on awakening and the writing of this book.

I was raised in Melbourne, Australia. After graduating from high school, I attended the University of Melbourne where I obtained a law degree. Shortly after graduating, I was on my way to Europe for an extended vacation. I loved it so much that I remained in Europe for almost five years, working in London whenever I needed to earn money. Eventually, I returned to Australia. I had already completed my law degree and so I decided to begin my law career as a barrister, complete with wig and gown and I chose to specialize in criminal law.

After several years, I realized that this was not my true calling and so I resigned. I did not know what would come next, but I knew that two things were important to me, creativity and communication. I allowed these two words to guide me into my future. About six months later, I got a job as a writer for an advertising agency.

I enjoyed my work with the agency because it involved both creativity and communication, which were so important to me. However, after about 18 months, I decided that this was not the right path for me and so I resigned. Once again, I did not know what would come next.

During that time I had become interested in meditation and personal growth. In December 1981, I decided to attend a seven-day personal growth retreat near Bellingen in Australia. I did not know any of the other participants in the group, nor did I know anything about the group leader. I really just wanted a vacation and an opportunity to meet some new friends.

The retreat was wonderful. I participated fully in the processes and I gained a great deal during those seven days. But much more significantly, it led to my first awakening and it was the first time that I had a direct experience of God. It was during this first awakening that God asked me to tell the truth about Jesus.

Three years would pass before I experienced the second awakening. It was during this second awakening that the truth about Jesus was revealed. Although these revelations affirmed the divinity of Jesus at a very deep level, they differed quite dramatically from traditional Christian beliefs.

There have been six of these awakening experiences, each more powerful than the one before and they occurred approximately every three years, beginning in 1981. I have included a fairly detailed description of my awakening experiences in Part 1 of this book.

It took many years before I felt comfortable sharing these revelations about Jesus. I have no intention or desire to offend anyone. Nor am I trying to persuade anyone of anything. If someone is happy with their religious beliefs, then I am happy for them. This book is not meant for them. But there are so many people who have turned away from religion. Many have chosen to be agnostic or an atheist.

Others have turned towards the East or to other spiritual disciplines looking for answers.

They are seekers, genuinely looking for meaning in their lives. I have written this book for them, and for anyone else who has an open mind and is willing to have their beliefs challenged in a way that leads to transformation.

The content of this book is very provocative. I do not ask you to believe one word that I have written. Belief is a function of the mind. There is no truth in belief. But as you read through the pages, if you can relate to what I am saying and it seems true, then I invite you to trust that.

When you are in the mind, you rely on concepts, opinions, beliefs and understanding to navigate through life. In Presence, all those things are replaced by an inner knowing. The truth is that you are already a fully awakened Being. You always have been. You always will be. But to the extent that you become absorbed into the past and future world of the mind, you disconnect from the truth that is always present within you.

The truth exists within each one of us. It does not belong to me and it does not belong to you. It belongs to God and is available equally to all, but only when we are present. So let's embark together on a wonderful journey, a journey of awakening. If enough of us awaken, our world will be transformed.

PART 1

LIBERATING JESUS

AWAKENINGS

THE FIRST AWAKENING

In December of 1981, I decided to attend a week-long personal growth retreat near Bellingen in Australia. The retreat was wonderful. I participated fully in the processes and I gained a great deal during those seven days. On the last day of the retreat, I had my first awakening. Nothing in my life could have prepared me for what I was about to experience.

Several interesting things happened during this retreat that I believe contributed to this first awakening. One day, a group of about eight of the participants were sitting by a tree during one of the morning breaks. One of the men in the group pulled out a book and said that he would like to read a paragraph from the book. His name was Kevin and I recall that the title of the book was *The Man* by Irving Wallace.

He began to read the paragraph and as he did so I broke down into uncontrollable tears. When he finished reading the paragraph, I had no clue what he had read and why it had affected me so deeply. I asked him to read the paragraph again. He did so and I broke down again. Still I did not know what he had read or why it had affected me. This was repeated at least five times. I then asked him to read the paragraph very slowly. Finally, I could hear the words and I knew what he had read.

I believe the quote was as follows,

"All man's honors are small beside the greatest prize to which he may and must aspire--the finding of his soul, his spirit, his divine strength and worth--the knowledge that he can and must live in freedom and dignity--the final realization that life is not a daily dying, not a pointless end, but a soaring and blinding gift snatched from eternity."

For some reason, these words opened up a very deep wound within me that I had lived with all my life. It was the feeling that I did not fit in, that I did not belong and that I had lived a life according to other people's values and expectations. As all the repressed pain surfaced within me, I knew that it was the beginning of a profound healing. Suddenly I knew where I belonged. It is in the present moment and I had the overwhelming feeling that the present moment was my true home.

The second significant thing that happened during the retreat occurred several days later. The group was sitting in a circle. Somehow the issue of judging one's self and others arose as a topic of discussion. I raised my hand and shared that I was very judgmental of myself. The group leader knew that I had been a lawyer, so he suggested that I prosecute myself and that the group would be the jury, who would then pass judgment upon me.

I definitely rose to the occasion. I had been a good lawyer and so I made a very strong case against myself. I shared all the things I thought were wrong with me. I shared all the judgments I had of myself. I was ruthless. After about ten minutes, I rested my case. I was absolutely convinced that I would be found guilty and that I would be condemned. To my utter surprise, the jury handed down its verdict.

"Not only do we find you not guilty, but we love you!"

Once again I collapsed into tears. Since that moment until the present day, judgment of myself and others simply dissolved.

Several more days would pass until we reached the last day of the retreat. At the end of the retreat, I went down to the river. We had swum there every day, enjoying the cool, fast-flowing water. There were some rapids in front of where I was standing and just beyond the rapids was a deep swimming hole. On the other side of the river, the densely forested bank rose sharply upwards towards the sky. With the sun warming my body, I stood on the bank of the river appreciating the natural beauty of my environment.

Suddenly, I found myself being taken through a spontaneous meditation which unfolded in stages over the next fifteen or twenty minutes. I didn't know what was happening or what I was doing. In a way, the meditation was being done to me. Each sequence of the meditation was spontaneous and unplanned. It was as though, in some mysterious way, I was being guided from another dimension. I felt my arms opening and for about ten minutes, I stood with arms outstretched embracing the trees on the opposite bank of the river with my consciousness. I became very present with the trees and quite literally took the energy and consciousness of the trees into me. I became one with the trees.

After about ten minutes, I walked slowly into the river. The day before, it had been raining and the river was quite high. The waters before me flowed rapidly over the rocks. It was a little difficult to gain a foothold, but I managed to walk into the river where the rapids were at their strongest. The water was about chest high or perhaps a little lower.

I turned to face the force of the flowing river.

Under normal circumstances, it would have been difficult to stand against the rapids. But I had the trees within me. I felt incredible power and strength and stability within me. I defied the rapids. I defied the river with my strength and my will. I was in total inner silence. It was as though I was revealing my true self to the river. I felt completely exalted. I stood against the rapids for about ten minutes. Then without thinking, I took three or four strong strokes through the rapids to the deep swimming hole, which lay just beyond.

Spontaneously, I dived deeply. The swimming hole was dark and murky and I had the sense that I was diving into the very depths of darkness. As I surfaced from the depths and arose out of the water, I let out a sound which I can only describe as a primal roar. This primal roar filled the whole valley as it emerged from deep within me. It seemed like a declaration that I had finally arrived. I repeated this process three times, each time emerging from the water with a primal roar.

I then took three or four strokes forward into the heart of the rapids and surrendered to the river. I let go completely and was carried away. My eyes were closed. I was face down. I was carried over rocks. I gave no thought whatsoever to protecting myself. I could easily have been injured. I could easily have been dashed against the rocks and knocked unconscious. But I surrendered. I trusted the river completely. I came to rest in a still part of the river about one thousand feet downstream.

As I made my way to the riverbank, I could tell that I was in a completely different dimension. I was in an altered state of consciousness. It was my first experience of the awakened state, although I had no idea at that time what was happening to me. The sum total of my past experiences could not provide any kind of explanation for what I was experiencing as I emerged from the river.

Time had disappeared. I was overwhelmed with a sense of love and Oneness. I was overwhelmed with a sense of the sacred and the divine. Everything seemed perfect to me. I was in a state of total bliss. Magic was in the air as I set off along the gravel road that ran beside the river.

I had awakened into a world of extraordinary beauty and I felt completely intoxicated with divine love. I found myself saying, "I love you" over and over again. I could not stop myself. I told the cows that were grazing in the meadow that I loved them. I told the trees that I loved them. I told the sky and the clouds and the river that I loved them. Songs of love, which I had never heard before, began pouring out of me.

One song that emerged surprised me.

"The river Jordan is deep and wide. Found my love on the other side."

I repeated that song many times singing to the birds and the trees and the flowers. Everything I saw and heard was embraced by my love. I felt like Saint Francis of Assisi. I was consumed with love. I was devoured by love. I was intoxicated with love. Everything in existence was perfect. I was filled with a sense of wonder and amazement.

Eventually, I returned to the retreat center. I walked into a room where many of the group participants were relaxing at the end of the day. When I walked into the room, I had a very strange and somewhat unsettling experience. People were laughing and talking but as I looked at them, I could very clearly see a face behind the face they were presenting. It was as if everyone was wearing a mask. It was a little too much for me at that time, so I left the room and walked back along the road beside the river.

After a while, I began to receive a flow of insights and revelations about the nature of the human condition. It was becoming clear to me how and why humanity had gone so far astray. Some significant keys to spiritual awakening were being revealed. My consciousness was opening up to the wisdom of the ages. It was an exhilarating experience.

Just then, the energy changed. The level of love and light in everything around me dramatically increased. I sensed a Presence within me and all around me that I had never experienced before. I do not know how, but I knew instantly that it was God.

Suddenly and without warning, God spoke to me.

"Tell the truth about Jesus!"

I could not tell whether the voice of God was coming from within me or outside of me. Up until this point in my life, I had been an agnostic. I could not accept a God who had allowed so much suffering in the world. But this was a God of love and perfect compassion. I was being asked by God to tell the truth about Jesus. And I was being asked to speak publicly about it.

I did not know what God was talking about.

"I do not know the truth about Jesus!" I cried. "And even if I did know,
I would be too afraid to speak about it publicly!"

"As you wish my beloved," was God's loving reply.

God's response to me was overwhelming. I had never before experienced such a level of love and acceptance. This was truly a God of love. This was an allowing God. I was even allowed to refuse God's request. I was still in an exalted state of love and bliss. I was in the eternal realm in which time seemed to have no place. I saw beauty and Oneness in everything.

The next morning it was time to leave the retreat center. I gathered my belongings together and headed for my car which had remained in the parking area since my arrival. Something very strange happened when I got into the car. I placed the key in the ignition but I did not know what to do. I had forgotten how to drive a car. It was as if the past had been completely removed from my consciousness. I turned the key and the engine started. I tentatively put my hands on the steering wheel and my foot on the accelerator and to my amazement, the car began to move in a forward direction. Slowly my ability to drive came back to me. I headed off at a very slow speed, with absolutely no idea where I was headed.

After about thirty minutes, I came to a T-intersection. I did not know which way to go, so I turned left. That did not feel right so I made a U-turn and headed in the opposite direction, still not knowing which way to go. It was not long before I was completely lost.

I stopped the car and immediately heard a voice say, "Write!"

I pulled out a pen and a notebook and began writing. I must have filled up at least ten pages of that notebook. By the time I had finished writing, I was so disturbed by what I had written that I tore each page into the smallest of pieces. I was absolutely determined that no one should ever see what was written on those pages. Unfortunately, I have no memory of what I wrote, although I have the feeling that God had been dictating the words to me. The content of that material was simply too much for me to accept at that time.

If I have any regret in my life, it would be the shredding of the pages of that notebook.

Gradually, I was being returned to a more manageable and peaceful state. It was time for integration. Over the next few days I visited several friends in the area. I then headed south to join a friend. I was still in an awakened state of consciousness, but I had come down from the peak of the
experience considerably.

Three years would pass before I experienced the second awakening. It was during the second awakening that I opened into the eternal dimension of existence. It was during the second awakening that the truth about Jesus was revealed. It was during the second awakening that I entered fully into the experience of Heaven on Earth.

THE SECOND AWAKENING

It had taken three years to integrate the experience of that first awakening. During that time, I read extensively and visited several Masters in India in an endeavor to understand what had happened to me. Gradually, I was returned to the Oneness and love that I had experienced three years earlier, but it was much softer and I was able to function more easily in the world.

In December of 1984, I returned to the Jasmine Retreat Center, where I had experienced my first awakening. This time I was running the retreat. There were about thirty people in attendance and most of them had worked with me for over a year. It was a very powerful event and almost everyone opened into the deepest levels of awakened Presence. There were a number of very powerful healings that occurred during this retreat, including some very powerful past life healings.

With each passing day of the retreat, I was becoming more present. I was opening once again into the eternal dimension. I was opening into Oneness. Time had disappeared and I knew that I was entering into another peak experience. This one seemed even more powerful than the first. I experienced Oneness with everything I encountered. It was magical. It was full of mystery and wonder. I was in a state of perfect silence, Presence and love. The trees, the flowers, the birds, and even the insects were experienced as loving friends, sharing this beautiful world with me.

On the last day of the retreat, I lay down on the grass to rest. I closed my eyes, stretched my arms out wide and relaxed deeply. I could hear the sound of the river in the distance. I could hear birds singing. My mind was silent and I was in a state of perfect Presence. Then, all of a sudden I found myself transported through time into another dimension. Somehow I was on the cross, experiencing the crucifixion in perfect detail. It was as though I was looking through the eyes of Jesus, hearing all the sounds and feeling all the feelings involved in that experience.

I felt the physical pain of the crucifixion and I experienced that terrible moment on the cross when he cried out, "My God, My God, why hast thou forsaken me?"

Then followed a series of revelations about what really happened to Jesus on the cross and what has happened to him since his death. This process of revelation unfolded over the next few days. I was in several different realms of consciousness at the same time. It was very confusing and quite a difficult experience to go through. I felt overwhelmed by these revelations. Although they affirmed the divinity of Jesus at the deepest level, nevertheless there were some startling departures from traditional Christian beliefs.

By the time this awakening began to subside, I was completely exhausted. I had not slept for many nights, nor had I eaten much. Some close friends drove me to Byron Bay and I stayed in a cabin behind their house. I collapsed into bed and slept for three days. When I awakened, I was in Heaven on Earth.

It is difficult to describe what it was really like. I can only say that I no longer existed as an individual. I had been completely absorbed into Oneness. My mind was utterly silent. The past and future had disappeared. Quite literally, there was no life outside the present moment and there was nothing of me outside of the present moment.

The cabin was set in a beautiful forest. It was quiet and secluded and all I could hear was the sound of birds singing. For the next three weeks, I lay in bed or sat in a chair by the window, totally immersed in the mystery of existence. Occasionally, I went for a walk, but my body was quite weakened by the experience.

I had very few visitors during this time, and the few that did come did not really know how to be with me. I was not able to engage in conversation, but if anyone asked a question or sought guidance, I could respond.

I was in a constant state of profound love and Oneness. Then one day, these words spontaneously arose from deep within me.
"No one will come!"

Somehow these four words conveyed a message to me. I must come down from the mountainous heights of consciousness that I was on and return to a more normal level. Then I could function in the world of time and make myself available to others seeking guidance.

"If no one would come to me, then I would go to them."

It was difficult to come down from that peak, but after about three months I was able to resume a life within the world of time. I had no expectation or desire for any more awakenings. I was more than content to live a quiet and peaceful life, going for walks, sipping tea in the local cafes of Byron Bay, and sharing the teaching with those who found their way to me. In December of 1990, I scheduled a residential retreat, once again at the Jasmine Retreat Center. I was about to enter into my third awakening.

THE THIRD AWAKENING

It was a seven-day retreat and once again, I began to open into the eternal dimension of existence. I was taken on a journey through the mystery of existence. I became the rocks and the trees and the birds and the sky. I journeyed through time from the beginning to the end and from the end to the beginning. I experienced God in everything. I felt the Presence of Buddha and Jesus. I was in the company of saints and sages. It was profoundly mysterious. I was completely absorbed into Presence and Is-ness. In a sense, I ceased to exist as a separate individual. There was nothing of me from the past or the future. Once again, I found myself in Heaven on Earth.

If I reflect upon the earlier experiences, I would say that the first awakening was a massive opening of the heart. The second was an opening into Christ consciousness. The third was an awakening into God consciousness. After several weeks, the awakening gradually subsided and it took many months of integration before I could resume a normal life.

THREE MORE AWAKENINGS

There have been three more awakenings. The fourth occurred in 1992 and lasted only a week. It involved revelations about the nature of love and what it means to live lovingly in the world. The fifth awakening occurred in New York City during the summer of 1995. It was an integration of all the other awakenings. As I wandered the streets of Manhattan, in a completely altered state of consciousness, everything seemed to fall into place. All the insights and revelations of my earlier awakenings collapsed into a single point. Sacred geometry arose within my consciousness, somehow revealing the origins of our existence. Once again, I experienced Oneness with everything I encountered. But this time it was with cars and buses and lamp posts, rather than trees and flowers and the river. Everyone I saw looked enlightened to me. I could see that we are all brilliant actors playing out roles upon some cosmic stage.

After the fifth awakening, I was sure that it was over and that my journey was complete. I did not expect anything more and then without warning, the sixth awakening occurred in May of 1997.

I had traveled to Michigan to run a weekend workshop in Ann Arbor. I was staying with a friend when the sixth awakening began to open up within me. I found myself in the company of ascended Masters, most notably the legendary Mahavatar Babaji, but also many others.

During this sixth awakening, which lasted for about fourteen days, I felt like an immortal. I was very connected to the stars and to space. I was in a continual state of rapture. One of the primary features of the sixth awakening was an overwhelming and intense feeling of love and compassion for all animals. There was a farm nearby and each morning I would walk there and spend time with the geese and peacocks wandering freely around. There were also goats, cows and very large horses grazing in the greenest paddocks. I felt so much love for them that I could hardly bear it.

One day, it occurred to me that I wanted to see other animals. I wanted to see lions and tigers and gorillas. I wanted to see zebras and giraffes and so my friend drove me to the nearest zoo which was about two hours away. We arrived before the gates opened and waited for almost an hour. When at last we entered, the first exhibit we saw was that of the gorillas. They were in a large grassy enclosure. In the distance, I could see a large male gorilla standing next to a smaller female. There were also two or three young gorillas and a baby.

I walked over to the viewing area. A large glass panel provided a clear view of the gorillas who were gathered together in the far corner of the enclosure. I was in a deep state of loving Presence as I stood behind that glass wall. Slowly, the female gorilla began to walk towards me. With each step she took, I became more present. She gazed directly into my eyes as she approached and to my surprise, she sat down right in front of me and placed her hand on the glass, as if to greet me.

I was filled with love for her in that moment. She truly was a magnificent and present Being. I placed my hand on the glass opposite hers and we entered into the deepest level of communion. Gazing into her eyes was like gazing into eternity. We remained in a state of silent communion for at least ten minutes. I found myself speaking to her.

"I love you," I repeated over and over again.

And then the deepest level of sorrow arose within me.

"I am so sorry," I told her. "I am so sorry for what we have done to you."

It felt like I was speaking to all gorillas through her. How could we be so cruel and destructive in our unconsciousness? The deep remorse that was arising within me was not enough to overwhelm the love

I felt for her. I just sat with her, telling her over and over again that I loved her, and that I was sorry. Our communion continued for another five minutes and then, to my amazement, the baby gorilla slowly approached, sat down next to his mother, looked right into my eyes and raised his hand to meet mine.

I spent the next fifteen minutes, hand to hand, with mother and child. The only thing between our hands was a thin layer of glass. Gazing into the baby's eyes was like gazing into an ocean of innocence.

After a while, other humans began to gather around to watch what was happening. They were talking and laughing and it was clearly time to disengage. I said good-bye to the gorillas and decided to leave the zoo. I returned to my friend's home and remained in a fully awakened state for several more weeks. I will never forget that time I spent in Holy Communion with the gorillas at the Toledo Zoo.

After this final awakening settled, I spent the following years traveling from place to place. I would simply go wherever I was invited. It was not long before I began receiving invitations to share my teaching in numerous locations in the United States and around the world.

AUTHOR'S NOTE

Many years would pass before I had the courage to speak openly about my awakenings and the revelations about Jesus. I really did not want to offend anyone and yet God's request to tell the truth about Jesus was always there in the background. Even though I had been sharing my teaching on awakening in many different countries over the years, I always felt that sooner or later I would have to do what God asked of me. It occurred to me that an effective and less challenging way to share the truth about Jesus would be to present the revelations in the form of a play, which I called Liberating Jesus.

It took me about a year to write Liberating Jesus. I then performed the play in 2006 in Los Angeles for six weeks. It was rather challenging as I had no experience in the theater, and I found myself playing the role of writer, producer, assistant director, actor and make-up person. It was rather stressful, but it worked out well and the audience seemed to respond favorably.

I was delighted that the play was so well received. After the play ended in Los Angeles, I was invited to perform the play in Kansas City at the Unity Village, before an audience of almost 500 people. Once again the play was well received. I was quite relieved as there were many Unity Church ministers in attendance.

After each performance of the play, I came back on stage and answered questions from the audience. The questions were sometimes about Jesus and the content of the play, but they were also about awakening and Presence in a more general sense. I trust that the questions and answers will provide clarity and guidance for anyone on a path of awakening. My intention in writing this book was simply to complete what God had asked of me many years ago during my first awakening.

I am also aware that some people might like to study the words in the play more closely and so I have included the script of the play for those who are interested.

The play was filmed and is now available for viewing at www.leonardjacobson.com/liberatingjesus.

A word of caution: If you are a Christian who adheres to traditional Christian beliefs, rituals and practices, you probably should not read beyond this point or watch the movie. I have no intention or desire to offend anyone.

PART 2

LIBERATING JESUS

THE SCRIPT OF THE PLAY

THE SCRIPT OF THE PLAY

Cast of Characters: *Jesus, God, Satan, the ego, Abraham (all played by Leonard)*

Setting: *Black curtains surround the stage and the floor is black, giving the impression of a void, shrouded in darkness. There is a small table on the left and right sides of the stage, with a beautiful arrangement of flowers on each table. Further back, there are two more small tables on the left and right side of the stage, with 5 large candles on each table. The candles are unlit.*

Introductory music *is played about 15 minutes before the play commences. The house lights are up. An overhead light is on. The house lights fade, signaling that the play is about to start. The stage is in darkness. The music changes. As the music is playing, Jesus walks to center stage. It is still dark. The lights fade up, revealing Jesus. It is not Jesus from the past, but rather Jesus as he is today, returned to set the record straight. He is dressed casually. His manner is friendly, yet intense. Even in silence, his Presence engages the audience at a very deep level.*

Throughout the play, there are pauses in his monologue. During each pause, there is a short musical interlude of between 20-30 seconds.

Jesus begins to speak.

LIBERATING JESUS

ACT 1

John the Baptist once declared that there is one coming who will take away the sin of the world. I wonder if he knew what that really meant and how long it would take me to fulfill his prophecy.

I recall meeting him by the river Jordan. He spoke in a way that excited me. Something deep within me was stirred. He was baptizing people in the water. He held their heads under the water for a long time, almost to the point where they could die for lack of breath. As soon as they struggled, he would release them and they came out of the water, gasping for breath and for life.

I could not really see the point to it, but I stepped forward and I too was immersed in the water. I had decided not to struggle. I trusted that this man would not let me die. I was held under the water for a long time. It seemed like forever. I wanted to struggle but then I felt myself surrender.

"If I am to die, then so be it," I said to myself.

I felt myself passing into endless darkness. I was disappearing into nothingness. I surrendered completely. At last my head was lifted out of the water. I opened my eyes and looked around. Everything looked completely new and fresh. It was as if everything was lit from within and filled with the Presence of God. It was the same world I had lived in just moments before my immersion in the water, but it felt like I was seeing it for the first time. For the first time, I was fully present and awake in the truth of life and I could feel the Presence of God in everything.

John smiled at me. "I love you," he said.

We embraced and then I left. I knew I had to walk alone into the desert. Something new and beautiful had awakened within me, but first I knew I had to purify myself. I set off into the desert without food and only a little water. The days were long and extremely hot. The nights were cold and lonely. In all this time, I hardly slept. I was extremely tired and yet I felt completely awake. I had lost track of the days and nights. Then, one late afternoon as the sun was setting, I had a vision. Satan appeared before me in the desert. He had come to tempt me. He had come to claim me as his own.

"Why do you go hungry?" Asked Satan. "If God is with you, then just turn these stones into bread. Feed yourself."

"Bread can fill my body," I answered. "But only God can fill my life. I will not use the power of God to feed myself."

"Prove to me who you are!" Said Satan. "Cast yourself from the highest temple. If God is truly with you, then you will not be harmed."

"I will not put God to the test," I replied. "God does not have to prove anything to you."

"I offer you power and glory and the riches of all the kingdoms if you will but serve me," said Satan.

"I serve only God," I answered and with that Satan was gone.

My encounter with Satan was extremely useful. I was purified of any unconscious or hidden desires. It had become clear that I would not misuse the power of God in any way and that I would not succumb to the desire for personal power and recognition. As soon as Satan was sure that I was a true Servant of God, I was released from further temptation.

(Lights fade, music plays)

After my sojourn in the desert, the Presence of God filled me completely. I gathered together a small number of people and we began roaming the countryside. I shared my simple message with all those who could hear.

"The Promised Land which you seek is here now. Open your eyes and you will see it. God is within you and the time of deliverance is now."

I traveled the countryside speaking the words as they arose within me. Many wanted to be healed, but very few could hear my simple message. For the truth has no power to penetrate into the world of belief. Belief must dissolve of its own accord before the truth will enter.

Almost everyone I encountered was lost in the world of the mind. They were so used to living in the past and future that they could not respond to my invitation into the present moment. There was so much hurt and pain and anger repressed within them, that they could not respond to love. They were so firmly locked into their opinions and beliefs that they could not respond to truth. Only a small number responded to my call to Presence. Most were indifferent. And a few were so threatened by my words and by my Presence that they crucified me.

And I am still on the cross. Your need for me to be crucified for your sins has kept me on the cross for almost two thousand years. Don't you think that is enough for anyone? Is that what you really want? To hold me eternally imprisoned within that moment of time when I died on the cross. I am so tired of being on this cross. How long must I suffer for your sins?

(Lights fade, music plays)

I never intended to be your Savior. Why would you want me to save you? Don't you want to take responsibility for yourself? Don't you want to take responsibility for your thoughts, feelings and actions? If I am your Savior, I deny you the opportunity to embrace true responsibility, which is a prerequisite for awakening into the truth of life and Oneness with God.

I have come back. It has taken me two thousand years, but I have come back. I had no choice. I have to straighten things out. There has been so much misunderstanding. Or worse than misunderstanding, my words and the story of my life and death were deliberately altered after my death to attract followers.

Not everything in the New Testament is accurate, but if you know how to distinguish truth from fiction, then what I said then and what I am saying now can have a profoundly liberating effect upon you. But it is up to you, not me!

I told my disciples that not every one will be able to hear the truth. I said it in many different ways.

"Those with ears to hear, let them hear."

That was my favorite expression.

I knew that my teaching was not for everyone. I was sent to find those who were ready to respond. God told me that I would know them by their response. And the same is true now. I shall know you by your response. I am like a sower, sowing a seed. With some people, there is little chance of anything changing. They are too locked into their beliefs. Their minds are too rigid. Their fear of uncertainty is too strong to allow the truth to enter. They are too defended. They are like stony ground.

But what is the point of a Messiah who brings to you a message that you already know? It was because my message contradicted your beliefs that you crucified me. Please don't make that mistake again. But there are many in this audience who I call the 'good ground.'

You are prepared. Your soul is mature. You have longed for God and Oneness for many lifetimes and you are ready for the truth. When it appears, you will know it within yourself, for the truth can only be known from within and at the deepest level, it is known in silence. My Presence is an invitation for you to be fully present and awake in the truth of life. You will not find the truth threatening. You will experience it as liberating. It is what you have been searching for. Your heart will dance and sing in celebration.

Which are you, stony ground or fertile soil? Which are you? Which are you? Which are you? For I have much to share with you, my Beloveds. And very little time.

(Lights fade, music plays)

With your permission, I want to share with you a fundamental correction. Your belief in sin is false. It's an illusion that has arisen in your mind, but it keeps you locked in guilt and separation. And it keeps me nailed upon the cross!

The only real sin is the sin of your unconsciousness. The only real sin is to be lost in the past and future world of your mind, believing in it as the truth of life. The only real sin is to believe in your beliefs, including your belief in God. How much cruelty have we perpetrated upon each other in the name of our beliefs?

If we are not truly present, then we don't know who we are. We don't know where we are and we don't know God. To believe in God is a very poor substitute for knowing God. God is real. God is here now. But we are not. We have gone too far into a world of illusion, made real through the power of belief. We have wandered too far from the present moment, which is the only truth of life. What can God offer you, other than what is here with you in this moment? Like the prodigal sons and daughters of God, we have taken ourselves into a world of separation and illusion, and now we are lost there. And we have no sense of the implications of this simple truth. It is the sole cause of all suffering. Don't you know who you are? You are the sons and daughters of God. Don't you know where you are? This is Heaven on Earth, and it is such a blessing to be here on earth.

(Lights fade, music plays)

I am not your Savior, at least not in the way you think I am. And I did not die for your sins. But I did fall for your only sin, which is the sin of unconsciousness, and it has been a difficult journey since my fall upon the cross.

Let me take you through the whole experience of the crucifixion, all the way up to that point when I cried out to God, "Why hast thou forsaken me?" Prior to that moment, I was not in distress. Even though I had been brutalized and even though I was in great pain, I was connected to God. I could feel God's Presence and God's love and it sustained me. I was in Oneness with God. I was in a state of trust and surrender to the will of God.

But then everything changed!

I looked out into the crowd and I saw despair. My mother was there. She was weeping. Magdalene was there with some of my closest disciples. They were all weeping. And somehow it caught me. I got involved in their despair. And at that point, I fell. It was a fall in consciousness. Suddenly, the light of God began to fade. I could feel the Presence of God leaving me. The physical pain flooded in. I was overwhelmed with despair and confusion.

What had I done wrong?
Had I failed God in some way?
Had I loved these people too much?
Had I told them more than I should have?
Had I misled them in some way?

All these questions arose in an instant.

I looked out and all I could see was despair. I looked down and unimaginable terror arose within me. For the very earth seemed to open up beneath me. Human unconsciousness, like a thousand snakes in a bottomless pit, rose up to swallow me. I was about to fall into eternal darkness. I was filled with the suffering of an unconscious humanity.

"My God, my God! Why hast Thou forsaken me?" I cried.

And then I died.

(Lights fade, music plays)

There was no resurrection. What happened to me next is not known to Christians or anyone else. Christians believe that I surrendered to the death of my physical body and died for their sins. But my crucifixion was not about my physical death. I was not afraid of dying. I was way beyond identification with my physical body. The death of my physical body and the pain and suffering I endured on the cross was not the true sacrifice. It was not the true passion.

I was about to become the Lamb of God in a way that few people could possibly realize. Even I did not know what would happen next. My short visit upon the earth had failed. It was such a simple plan. I would walk upon the earth and God's Presence within me would be enough to awaken those around me. My teaching would be clear and irresistible to those with ears to hear. But the resistance was too strong. People were so lost that they could not respond. They could not awaken. Even my disciples could not accept that the feeling of God and love and Oneness that they experienced in my Presence was arising within them and was not coming from me. They projected it all onto me and saw me as the doorway to God. That is not what I intended. I came to reflect to them who they are. I came to reveal to them where God is.

If in my Presence you feel love, it is because you are love. If in my

Presence you feel God, it is because God is within you. All that I am, you are.

But they could not accept it. They felt unworthy. They were too lost in the mind. That is why the fall on the cross was necessary. Someone would have to journey through the maze that is the world of the human thinking mind in an effort to find the way through. Many had tried before and had lost their way. Now I would have to embark upon that desperate journey into human unconsciousness. If only I could find the way through, then the Way would be revealed for others. It has been a difficult journey since my fall upon the cross, but it was a journey initiated by God in that moment of the fall.

(Lights fade, music plays)

It is difficult to understand, but in that moment of my fall upon the cross, there was a split in my consciousness. At one dimension of consciousness, I've been nailed onto the cross, enduring the pain and suffering involved in that moment of the fall. I've been held there by your need for me to be crucified for your sins and by your belief in me as your Savior. At another dimension, I've been journeying through human unconsciousness for two thousand years, lost within the world of the mind, trying to find the way through.

I have lived many lifetimes since my death upon the cross. I have experienced all the human emotions and every kind of suffering. I have experienced isolation and despair. I have encountered all the forms of cruelty and injustice known to man. I have experienced guilt and shame and judgment over and over again. I have experienced the pain of living in a world of separation, where no one is truly present. I have experienced the pain of separation from God, which is the true source of all pain and suffering. It seemed as though I was taking the pain and suffering of the whole world upon my shoulders. I was weighed down with the suffering of all humanity.

And there was no escape!

The realm of the human thinking mind is like an endless labyrinth. It is an intricate web of illusion from which there is no escape. I could not find the way out, no matter how hard I tried. I studied all the religious teachings. I followed all the spiritual paths. But still I could not find the way out. I had no idea who I'd been or why I'd come here.

With very little break between lifetimes, I've continued on my way, lost like everyone else, unable to find my way back to God. I had no way of knowing that in this lifetime I would be restored to God. I had no way of knowing that the split in my consciousness would be healed and that my pain and suffering would be turned so completely into love and compassion. I had no way of knowing that my feelings of isolation and separation would be turned so completely into Oneness and perfect union. I had no way of knowing that the time of the Resurrection is now.

(*Lights fade, music plays*)

In this lifetime, the Way of liberation has been revealed to me. I am restored to truth, love and Oneness. I am restored to my true home, which is the present moment. I am restored to God. The Savior has been saved. The fallen Jesus is resurrected. I did not die for your sins. I fell for your sin of unconsciousness, which is the only sin. Is that not a much greater sacrifice than dying for your sins? I truly was the Lamb of God!

I came as the Son of God. But now I come as the Son of Man, and my message has not changed.

'That which you seek is here now.'
'All that I am you are.'

When you awaken fully into Presence and the realization of Oneness with God you are a Christ, which simply means that you are awake in Oneness with God. You are the Savior, but only of yourself.

You have saved yourself and you have saved your soul by liberating yourself from the past and future world of the mind into the world of Now.

You have delivered your soul into its own immortality. That makes you a part of the second coming of Christ, and it matters not whether you are a Christian, a Buddhist, a Jew or a Muslim. In truth we are all One and there is only one God. The conflict that we experience with each other exists only because we are lost in the illusion of separation.

It is time for every Christian to become a Christ. And what I am sharing is not just for Christians. I was not a Christian. I was a Jew. I never considered myself to be anything other than a Jew. My mother was Jewish. My disciples were Jewish. Everything that occurred in my life was according to Jewish law and Jewish prophecy. I came to deliver a message for the Jews. I came to help them fulfill their Sacred Covenant with God, because they were lost.

It is important that Christians recognize and honor their Jewish origins. To understand what it means to be Jewish, you have to go all the way back to the covenant with Abraham. The covenant is simply this. "Enter into right relationship with me," says God, "and I will deliver you unto the Promised Land." That's it. That's all you need to know about what it means to be Jewish. The problem is that God did not reveal to Abraham some very important details.

For example,

What is the Promised Land?
Where is the Promised Land?
How do we get there?
How will we recognize it when we arrive there?
And what is right relationship with God?

Perhaps Abraham should have insisted on answers to these questions, for without answers to these questions it has been difficult for Jews to fulfill their Covenant with God.

But let's roll the clock back. Let's go back in time. Let's give Abraham an opportunity to ask these questions of God, for God's answers will provide clarity and guidance not only for Jews, but also for Christians and Muslims and any one else seeking to awaken.

How can I roll the clock back, you might ask? How can I go all the way back to Abraham? Well, let me say once again, "Before Abraham was, I am."

(Lights fade, music plays)

Now this is Abraham speaking.

"Beloved God, please tell me, what do you mean by the Promised Land?"

"Abraham, the Promised Land is a reflection of your consciousness. When you are fully present and awake in the truth of life, the Promised Land will be revealed. And when it is revealed, you will know it as Heaven on Earth, for Heaven revealed on Earth is the Promised Land."

"But God, where is the Promised Land?"

"It is right here, Abraham. It has always been here. It will always be here. Wherever you are, Abraham, it is always here."

"But I cannot see it."

"You cannot see it because you are not here yet, Abraham."

"I don't understand, God. If I am not here, then where am I?"

"Abraham, you are not here because you are lost in your mind. The world of the human thinking mind is an illusion. It is the only place where I do not exist Abraham, for I am not an illusion."

"Then where are you God? How can I find you?"

"I am always here, Abraham. I am in these flowers. I am in this table. I am in this room. I am the silent Presence at the very heart of all things present. I am the present moment, revealing its self to you right now. If you want to find me, you will have to come to where I am. You will have to bring yourself fully present, for I exist only in the present moment."

"But God, my thoughts never stop. I am always in the past or future. I don't know how to free myself from the mind."

"Be patient, Abraham. It will be revealed, if not to you then to those who will follow you. I will send a messenger of the Way."

"How will I know when I am in the Promised Land? How will I recognize it?"

"Your mind will be silent, Abraham. The past and future will dissolve and you will feel the deepest level of peace. It will feel like coming home. Everything you see will be alight with my Presence, and you will feel a kind of Oneness with all that is. Trust me Abraham, when you awaken unto the Promised Land, you will know."

"May I ask you one more question, God?"

"Of course you may, Abraham."

"What is right relationship with you, God?"

"To be present is to be in right relationship with me, Abraham. And as you deepen into Presence, you will gradually surrender to my will.

You will be motivated not by fear, but by love and a deep recognition of the Oneness of all things. Just be present Abraham, and you will know me and you will love me. That is all that is needed. Eventually, you will come to such a deep level of silence and Presence that the distinction between you and me will dissolve completely. All separation will dissolve and Heaven on Earth will be revealed. In that moment, you are no longer Abraham. You are Jacob, become Israel."

*(Stage lights fade. Jesus walks off stage. House lights fade up.
Intermission music fades up.)*

INTERMISSION

Before Act 2 begins, there is The Invocation.

THE INVOCATION

Intermission music fades to silence.
Jesus walks on stage towards the candles on stage left.
Lights fade up to where Jesus is standing and he begins to light the
candles. As he lights the candles, he speaks the following invocation.

I call upon Buddha to join me in this moment of Presence.
I call upon Krishna to join me in this moment of Presence.
I call upon Lao Tzu to join me in this moment of Presence.
I call upon Moses to join me in this moment of Presence.
I call upon Mohammed to join me in this moment of Presence.

Jesus walks to the table on the other side of the stage. As he lights each
candle, he continues with the invocation.

I call upon all the saints and sages who have ever lived to join me in
this moment of Presence. I call upon the Angels of God to join me
in this moment of Presence. I call upon Divine Mother and all the
awakened women who have ever walked upon this earth to join me
in this moment of Presence. I call upon each and every member of
this audience to join me in this moment of Presence.

For in truth, there is only one God and in Presence, we are all one.

(Lights fade, music plays)

ACT 2

I know that many await my Second Coming. Well, how do they think I am going to get here? Am I going to descend from the clouds on the wings of a dove? No! I've been on a long and difficult journey to get here. It is the same journey that everyone is on, and like everyone, I was lost. Lost in illusion, separate from God. And my past, like a dark and terrible secret, was buried deep within me.

In this lifetime, that past came flooding into my consciousness. I had to relive every terrifying moment, including my fall upon the cross and I can tell you, that was not easy. But now, I've remembered who I was and who I am, and why I am here.

During this lifetime, so much has been revealed to me about the nature of the mind and the existence of the ego. I have refined my teaching of the Way, so that now it is much more accessible. I no longer speak in parables. I want the meaning of my words to be clear and simple.

It might be difficult for some Christians to accept what I am saying. Unless I look exactly like the pictures of Jesus hanging on their walls or nailed onto their wooden crosses, they will not accept me. I would have to perform miracles before they will accept a revision of my teaching and agree to take me down from the cross. I would have to change water into wine and stones into loaves of bread. And that is not going to happen!

I have no interest in miracles. God does not have to prove anything. Either you respond to the truth or you don't. And you will be known by your response!

(Lights fade, music plays)

Now, with your permission, there are some things I need to clear up.

Let's start with Satan!

As you know, I encountered Satan in the desert. Satan tempted me and tried to test me. But it was not Satan. It was not the devil. I now know that it was my own ego, which somehow projected itself outside of me and took on the form of Satan.

Has anyone ever fasted for forty days and forty nights? Let me tell you what will happen if you do. You'll start hallucinating. You might even project your own ego outside of you. It was not Satan tempting me. It was not a devil. It was my own ego, but I did not realize it at the time. I thought it was some kind of devil but at least I could see and hear what it was up to, and I could say no to its temptations. If it had not been projected outside of me, it might have seduced or deceived me, and I could have been lost forever in a world of separation, a slave to my own ego.

I am very grateful now for that hallucination. It helped to create a space between the truth of me, which is who I am when I am silent and fully present, and my ego which is who I am when I am caught in the past and future world of the thinking mind.

I have come to realize that the resistance of the ego is the main obstacle to human awakening. The ego is the custodian of the separation. Its role is to keep you in a world of illusion, where it is in control. You have to be very careful. The ego is extremely skilled at pulling you out of the present moment. It presents its deception and seduction as your own thoughts, feelings, fears and desires. It is very easy to be deceived. Most of the time, there is no distinction between you and your ego and it has its way, without you ever knowing.

"Follow me," says the ego. "Come into my world of thought, memory and imagination where I am in control. Let me entangle you in a world of opinions, ideas, concepts and beliefs. Let me imprison you in your own past with blame, regret, guilt or resentment. Let me tempt you into the future with the promise of future fulfillment.

What does the present moment have to offer you? A few flowers! A candle! A darkened room! Come into my world. I can offer you so much more."

What is Satan other than the ego at a collective level? The ego is constantly tempting you out of the present moment and out of Oneness with God. If you are not careful, you will be lost forever in a world of illusion.

And that is exactly what has happened to humanity.

If you are to liberate yourself, you will have to get to know your own ego and how it functions. You will have to identify how it deceives you and that is only possible if you have awakened to a dimension of you which is transcendent of your ego. The only way to transcend the ego is to become so fully present that your thoughts stop and your mind is silent.

Only then can you be a witness to your ego.

Only then can you say,

"Get thee behind me. You little devil. You little trickster! You want to keep me in the mind, where you are in control. But you cannot deceive me any longer. I am awake now. And I am watching you always. You cannot escape my gaze, my friend."

You cannot defeat the ego. The ego thrives on judgment, rejection and struggle. The only thing that will bring the ego to a place of relaxation and surrender is the energy of love and acceptance. And that is not difficult if you are present, because when you are present, you are love. You are acceptance. Eventually, the ego will feel and trust the flowering of Presence within you and it will begin to relax. It will no longer fear Presence and it will no longer seek to pull you out of the present moment. When that happens, you are free.

To be awake and in Oneness with God simply means to be fully present in the moment of now. To be present is the simplest thing. It is your natural state. Every moment, you have a choice. Will you be present in the truth and reality of this moment or will you allow yourself to be seduced into the world of the mind?

Two thousand years ago, I cautioned you about the power of thought to lead you astray.

"Which of you by taking thought can add one cubit unto his stature? Therefore take no thought for tomorrow, saying what shall we eat? What shall we drink or how shall we be clothed? But seek ye first the kingdom of God, and all these things shall be added unto you."

If you do seek the Kingdom of God, then you will have to find your way into the present moment, for the present moment is the doorway to God. The present moment is God revealed. And if you find yourself at the deepest level of Presence, you will encounter the living Presence of God in all things present. What do you think Omnipresence means? For religious believers, it is a comforting concept. For mystics, who are fully present, it is a living reality.

Being present is remarkably simple. Just bring yourself present with something that is here in the moment with you. That is the simple key to liberation. If you can see it, hear it, feel it, taste it, touch it or smell it in this moment, then you can be present with it. And the moment that you are truly present, thoughts will stop. Your mind will fall silent. You will emerge from the past and future into the world of now.

The present moment is always calling for your attention. Every leaf moving on every tree is waving to you. It is saying, "Here I am. Will you not be present with me? Will you not see me?" Each flower is trying to attract you with its color and its beauty. "What more can I do?" Asks the flower. "Will you not see me? Will you not be present with me? Do you not know who I am? I am God in the form of a flower and I am trying to attract your attention."

In this moment, bring yourself present with your body as it breathes. Be present with the sound you hear in this moment. Be present with what you see. If you are moving, be present and conscious in the movement! Be present with whatever is here now. And when you are truly present, I can ask you, "Who is present in this moment?"

In Presence, you can answer, "I am! A silent Presence of pure consciousness! I am that eternal silent Presence of pure consciousness! I am that! I am."

This infinite and eternal silent Presence is the very essence of your Being. It is your true nature. It is that dimension of you which is of this moment and only of this moment. It is the Christ of you. It is the 'I AM' of you.

This leads me to the most important clarification that I have to share with you.

It is written in the New Testament that I said, "I am the way, the truth and the life. Only through me do you come to God." These two sentences form the foundation of Christianity. Never before in the history of the world have so few words led so many so far astray.

I did not say that. I could not say that. I would never place myself between you and God. God is within you. You cannot come to God through me. I have meditated on that sentence many times, feeling responsible for leading so many astray, but it is clear to me now what actually happened. In the reporting or translating of my words, they left out a word. One word is missing from that sentence, "I am the way, the truth and the life." If we place the missing word back in the sentence, then suddenly everything makes sense and Christians will be back on track. Only then will my words and my teaching have the power to awaken you. Just one simple word with two letters!

And the missing word is ….. "IS"

"I am IS the way, the truth and the life. Only through the I AM Presence do you come to God."

And I would hasten to add that the 'I AM' of me is within me but the 'I AM' of you is within you. How can it be otherwise? The way to God is not through me, but through the 'I AM' Presence within you. When you awaken fully into the present moment you are restored to life. And you are restored to Oneness with God.

(Lights fade, music plays)

I once uttered the following words,

"He that heareth my word is passed from death unto life. The dead shall hear my voice and they that hear shall live. The hour is coming in which all who are in their graves shall hear my voice."

On another occasion, one of my disciples wanted to stay behind to bury his father.

"Come follow me," I told him. "Let the dead bury the dead."

For me, if you were lost in the mind, unable to respond to my call to Presence, I referred to you as dead. That is what it felt like to me. However, if I referred to you as dead, then of course, it would take a resurrection to bring you to life. To be resurrected simply means to be restored to life. It means that you have arisen out of the dead world of the mind and now you are fully present. That is all I meant, but my use of the word resurrection led to myths about raising the dead and that has been a great distraction from my true teaching.

I am not responsible for those myths about raising the dead and the stories of miracles which I did not perform.

My disciples were trying to attract followers and without the myths and the stories of miracles, would anyone have been interested in my teaching after my death? I don't think so. How many would have been converted to Christianity over the centuries without myths and miracles to believe in? Won't anyone respond to the call to awaken without dressing it up with myths and miracles? Won't anyone choose to be present for no other reason than it is the truth of life? The myths and stories are for believers, who will not believe without myths and miracles to support their beliefs. Believers are like children, whose innocent minds have been contaminated with other people's stories.

I have such a problem with the word, 'belief.'

"He that believeth on me shall have everlasting life."

Did I say that? If I did, I am truly sorry. Believers will never awaken into the truth nor will they find God, nor will they have everlasting life. Wherever you see the word 'believeth' in the New Testament, please change it to 'respondeth.'

"He or she that respondeth to me, by awakening fully into the present moment, shall have everlasting life."

One who has everlasting life is one who has awakened so fully into the present moment that the eternal dimension of existence is revealed. It is time to let go of belief, for the truth is always beyond belief. I am not interested in believers. To believe or not believe is a function of the mind. There is no truth in belief. Belief imprisons you in a world of illusion. I am seeking those who can respond from within their own Being.

It is only through the direct experience of God and Presence that the truth can be known, and once you know, there is no need for belief. Bring yourself fully present.

God exists at the very heart of silence within you. When you are fully present, you open the door to God and God is revealed in everything.

You are the champions of God. You are the champions of your own soul. You are the redeemers of Oneness. You are the revealers of Heaven on Earth. Have you forgotten who you are?

(Lights fade, music plays)

The more present you are, the more the present moment will reveal its hidden treasures. However, there are many obstacles to becoming established in Presence.

The first obstacle arises out of your involvement in the past. I spoke of this two thousand years ago, but my words were so obscure that I don't think anyone really understood them. I told you then that whosoever is angry with his brother shall be in danger of the judgment. Therefore first be reconciled to your brother and then come and offer your gift before the Altar.

Now what is the judgment? It is not a judgment from God, for God is without judgment. The judgment is the movement from truth into illusion. It is the movement from Oneness into separation. It is the movement from Presence into the world of the mind. It is a fall in consciousness!

You bring the judgment upon yourself whenever you judge yourself or another. You bring the judgment upon yourself whenever you have unresolved feelings from the past repressed within you. You bring the judgment upon yourself whenever you lose yourself in others, and there are so many ways to lose yourself in others. You bring the judgment upon yourself whenever you are too involved in your own past. You will have to master the art of completing and releasing the past, for a past that is not reconciled will continually pull you out of Presence and Oneness with God.

And what is the gift that you bring to the Altar? It is the gift of your own Presence, which is the only gift you can bring to God.

The second obstacle to Presence arises out of your misunderstanding. I told you that whosoever shall smite thee on thy right cheek, turn to him the other also. Now why did I say that? I was not teaching you how to be good or righteous or submissive. I am not a moralist. When you are awake in the truth of life, there is no need for morality. The Ten Commandments are irrelevant. I was simply telling you to turn your cheek and not react to the one who struck you. If you react, you will be caught in that same level of unconsciousness as the one who struck you. You will lose yourself and you will lose your connection with the present moment. Respond rather than react. If you are present, your response will always be appropriate.

I also told you to love your enemies, bless those who curse you, do good to those who hate you, and pray for those who despitefully use you or persecute you. But I did not mean that you should repress feelings like hurt, anger or hatred. Everything I said about love was based upon you becoming present, for it is only when you are fully present that you *are* love. You cannot love your enemies, unless you are fully present. To attempt to do so is a lie.

Because of my teaching about love, there has been a tendency to present your self as loving and deny and repress feelings like hurt, anger and hatred. My words about love have created a kind of dishonesty. If you are not present, you cannot practice the truth of one who is present. This is where religions have gone astray. Religions are a collective attempt by those who are not present to practice the truth of one who is present. It will not work. When you repress your feelings and try to love those who have hurt you, your robes might be white but your heart and soul are full of darkness.

(Lights fade, music plays)

When you pray, do not pray in a way that separates you from God.

To be present is the highest form of prayer. It is like standing before God and whispering, "I am here now. Do with me as you will."

I told you how to pray. Do not be a hypocrite, praying in a way that others might see you. Enter into your closet and pray in secret. That means go within and pray. When you speak from Presence, your words flow into that infinite and eternal silence at the very center of your Being. That is where God is.

And what will you say to God?

If you are present, then more than likely the only thing you will say to God is "thank you."

And be prepared for God's response. It might arise in the form of words. Or it might arise as an intense feeling of love. Or it might arise as an overwhelming feeling of peace. The peace that 'passeth understanding.'

I also told you not to use vain repetitions. I gave you an example of how to pray, but I did not intend that it should be repeated over and over for thousands of years. You call it the Lord's prayer. I call it an example of how to pray.

"Give us this day our daily bread."

That's a clue! Focus on what you need for today. Don't go too far into the future for if you do, you will get lost there.

"Forgive us our trespasses, as we forgive those who trespass against us."

That's another clue. Through forgiveness, we release the past so that we are more available to the present moment.

"Lead us not into temptation, but deliver us from evil."

Now, what is the temptation? It is the temptation of our own egos. It is the temptation to leave the present moment and become absorbed into the past and future. It is the temptation into a world of separation and illusion. And what evil shall we be delivered from? The only evil is to be lost in the mind, believing in illusion as the truth of life. The only evil is to live unconsciously upon this earth.

And one more thing!

Wherever you see in the New Testament that I refer to God as my Father, please change that to God, my Father *and* my Mother. To refer only to the Father is out of balance within the world of duality. It is not complete. When the Mother is included, then we can transcend to the Oneness of God, transcendent of all duality. Only then is Oneness truly revealed.

It is time to awaken. We have gone too far into the world of the mind. We are too dominated by our own egos. We have become too empowered by our technology and too destructive to continue living unconsciously upon this planet.

It is now a question of survival. It will not be the meek who shall inherit the earth. It will be those who can respond to my call to Presence. It will be those who can liberate themselves from the past and future world of the mind. It will be those who can free themselves from the tyranny of the ego. It will be those who can arise in Presence and mastery.

I have come to reveal the way. It is the same way that I revealed two thousand years ago, but I had to simplify it so that it would be available to all those with eyes to see and ears to hear.

"Therefore whosoever hears these sayings of mine and follows them, I will liken him unto a wise man who built his house upon a rock. And the rain descended and the floods came and the winds blew and beat upon that house, but it fell not for it was founded upon a rock."

The present moment is like a rock. It is a solid foundation for your life within the world of time. Make the present moment the foundation of your life. Honor the present moment as the truth of life and the doorway to God. Only then will you become established in Presence.

Only then may you declare,

"God, it is accomplished. At last, I have come home. I am restored to Oneness and the truth of life. The river has returned to the ocean. Heaven on Earth is revealed.

And the angels sing, Hallelujah.

Center light remains on.
House lights come up a little more on the audience.

Hallelujah music fades in.

Jesus stands in Presence with the audience for one or two minutes.
When he brings his hands together in a prayer gesture,
the Hallelujah music fades.

All lights gradually fade to black.
Jesus leaves the stage.

The End

PART 3

LIBERATING JESUS

QUESTIONS & ANSWERS

QUESTIONS & ANSWERS

The play ran for six weeks at the Edgemar Center for the Arts in Santa Monica, California. After each performance, Leonard would leave the stage and then after about five minutes, he returned to answer questions from the audience. What follows is a record of some of those questions with Leonard's answers.

The questions cover a wide range of topics of great value to anyone on a path of awakening.

Question (female): I am not sure what you mean by being present. Can you tell me how to be present?

Leonard's Answer: It's so utterly simple. As I said in the play, just be present with something that is here in the moment with you. Pick any flower in this vase. Bring yourself very present with it, and just say 'yes' when you're present with it.

Female: Yes.

Leonard: Good, that's it. Now stay present with the flower for a few moments.

(A few seconds pass)

Now pick another flower and be present with that. Just say 'yes' when you're present with it. It's really simple.

Female: Yes.

Leonard: Good. Do you notice that in this moment that there are no thoughts?

Female: Yes.

Leonard: Good. Now, be present with your body breathing just for a few moments. Your body is breathing. That's all you need to know right now. Just say 'yes' when you're present with your body breathing.

Female: Yes.

Leonard: Good. Now be present with any sound you hear in this moment. Just say 'yes' when you're present with the sound.

Female: Yes.

Leonard: Do you see how simple it is? It's as simple as remembering to be present with what is here now. Every moment you have that choice. You can be present in the moment of now or you can drift off into the mind. When you drift off into the mind, you are entering into a world of illusion. You are leaving the world of here now and entering the world of not here. It is a world of past memories and future imaginings, together with all your opinions, concepts and beliefs.

Just notice when you drift off and gently bring yourself back to Presence. If you can see it, hear it, feel it, taste it, touch it or smell it, you can be present with it. The moment you are truly present, your thoughts will stop. You will emerge out of the past and future world of the mind into the present moment.

Be present when you are washing the dishes. Be present when you are putting the garbage out or when you're going for a walk. Whenever there is no need to be thinking, be present. And when it is appropriate to think, then think.

Question (female): Why would I choose to be present? What is the point to it?

Leonard's Answer: When you are present, you will feel

loving, peaceful and at ease. You will feel empowered and you will feel free. You might occasionally feel blissful, but that is not why you choose to be present. You choose to be present simply because the present moment is the only life really available to you. Everything else is past memory and future imagining. In truth, there is no life outside of this moment, so you are choosing to live in the truth of life rather than in a world of illusion. It is very simple. I can see that you are deepening into Presence right now. Does it feel peaceful?

Female: Yes!

Leonard: Just be here. I'm here, you're here! The flowers are here. That's all it is. As we deepen into Presence, Oneness is revealed. Heaven on Earth is revealed. To be present is your natural state. It's unnatural to be thinking all the time, but most people are unable to stop thinking.

Female: Thank you very much.

Leonard: You're welcome.

Question (female): I applaud your bravery in putting on this production. I think it's a tremendous effort.

Leonard: Thank you.

Question (female): In the play, however, you seem to be denying that Jesus performed miracles. That is troubling for me. I have experienced miracles in my lifetime. I have seen people heal. I have taken classes on healing, so why is it not possible that Jesus performed miraculous healings?

Leonard's Answer: Most of us live in abandonment of responsibility. We want someone to heal us or fix us. And yet to embrace true responsibility is one of the keys to awakening.

The idea that someone can save us, whether it is Jesus or anyone else is a perfect example of our not taking responsibility for ourselves.

Question: But what has that got to do with the miracles of Jesus?

Leonard's Answer: As I said in the play, the miracles are necessary to support Christian belief in Jesus as their Savior. The truth is that it does not matter whether or not Jesus performed miracles. Are there any reports of people awakening through his healing or his miracles?

Did anyone awaken to his level of consciousness? What is the point of healing without awakening? Most of the stories of miracles and myths about resurrection of the dead were invented after his death to attract followers. As I said in the play,

"How many would have been converted to Christianity over the centuries without the myths and stories of miracles to believe in?"

Even Buddhists invented stories around Buddha to attract followers. Won't anyone choose to be present for no other reason than it is the truth of life?

It is time to free ourselves from belief and awaken into the truth. Belief is for those who do not know God. Belief is a function of the mind. There is no truth in belief. Believers create God in their own image. One who knows God does not believe in God.

(Applause)

We can't afford to continue living unconsciously upon this earth. It is time to let go of spiritual concepts and beliefs. Our beliefs and our religions keep us in separation. It is only when we awaken into the very heart of silence that truth and Oneness will be revealed. Only when we are truly present will we experience the living Presence of God in all things present.

Question (male): In your book, *Journey into Now*, you talk about two steps to awakening. Could you speak about that?

Leonard's Answer: Yes. In my book, I describe it as a two-step dance of awakening. The first step involves being present. We must learn the art of being present. As I said earlier, just bring yourself present with something that is here in the moment with you. Being present is easy and immediate.

You cannot practice your way into Presence. You cannot be present at some time in the future. You can only be present now.

But remaining present in your day-to-day life and in your relationships is not so easy. Most of us are quickly pulled back into the world of the mind. That is why the second step is necessary. It involves bringing conscious awareness to all the ways that you are involuntarily pulled out of Presence. The first step leads to Presence. The second step leads to mastery of the mind and ego. Both steps are necessary for true awakening and liberation.

Male: Can you elaborate on the second step?

Leonard's Answer: There are four ways that we're pulled out of Presence and I'll speak about them briefly. The first is the resistance of the ego. The ego is extremely skilled at keeping you imprisoned within the mind. It has a bag of tricks to keep you in its world of the past and future, where it is in control. It keeps you in the past with thoughts and feelings like blame, anger, regret, resentment and guilt. These thoughts and feelings are just energies that arise from time to time and they arise with a story. In the story, someone is to blame for your unhappiness. You regret something that happened in the past. You feel guilty about something. You are resentful. Somehow the story justifies and validates the feeling.

But there is no truth in the story! Whatever happened is past and has nothing to do with this moment. By believing and identifying with the story you lock yourself into the past, which is what the ego wants.

The ego also has a remarkably clever trick to keep you imprisoned in the future. With one simple trick, the ego has managed to keep the whole of humanity out of the present moment and locked into an imaginary future. And what is that trick? It is the promise of future fulfillment. The truth is that you can never be fulfilled in the future. You can only be fulfilled now. It is a great lie. It is the ego's great deception. It will even promise you enlightenment at some time in the future, provided that you read certain books, visit certain teachers or engage in certain spiritual practices.

And the truth is that you'll never awaken or become enlightened in the future. It's not possible. The only moment you can ever be awakened is NOW. The good news is that NOW never goes away. It never gives up on you. It is constantly presenting you with opportunity after opportunity to come out of the dream and be present with what is here now.

If you want to release yourself from the past, then just notice these thoughts and feelings as they arise but do not believe in the story woven into the feeling. Do not be tempted into an imaginary future by the false promises of the ego. Bring it all to consciousness and then gently disengage from it.

The second way that we are pulled out of Presence is judgment and denial of who we have become on this long journey through time and separation. When you are present, you are love, you are acceptance and you are compassion. You are empowered from within. You exist in the realization of Oneness. You are pure consciousness itself. You are infinite and eternal. That is the truth of who you are!

But who have you become living lifetime after lifetime in a world where no one is present? Are you judgmental, critical and controlling? Do you feel unloved or alone? Do you feel unworthy? Are you angry, hurt or needy? Are you a victim? Are you looking for love or acceptance? Do you feel like a failure? Do you live with the limiting belief that you are not good enough? Do you live with fear?

Most of us are deeply committed to denying who we've become. We hide it, we project it onto others, we deny it. We try to fix ourselves, all of which implies judgment of who we have become. If you deny it, judge it or even try to fix or change who you have become, you are declaring that you believe in the dream and you are allowing the past to define you.

But if you own, acknowledge and confess who you have become, without judgment, it will gently open the door to the truth of who you really are. How can you be other than who you've become given the journey you've been on? How could you be other than who you have become given the parents you had and the circumstances of your childhood.

If you are to awaken, you will have to go through a process of owning, acknowledging and confessing who you've become, without judgment. Stop hiding it, stop being ashamed.

The third way we are prevented from being present has to do with repressed emotions. To the extent that we have emotions repressed within us from the past, how can we be present? Those repressed feelings are constantly being triggered by people and events in our life and when the emotions are triggered we are no longer present. We are caught in a painful past, which we project onto the present moment.

If you are to awaken, you will have to go through a process of allowing the repressed feelings from the past into conscious and responsible expression. Use every opportunity to allow those repressed emotions to arise and complete their journey through you.

You are present with the emotions as they arise. You experience them consciously, but you are not identified with the story woven into the feelings. You are simply the witness to these feelings arising. In order to complete this process, you will have to learn how to be in right relationship with the feelings as they arise, and you will have to learn how to experience and express the feelings consciously and responsibly.

The fourth way that we are pulled out of Presence is very interesting. In a way, we have to go through a process of separation to come to Oneness. We are all lost in each other. We are all entangled in each other. The moment you want someone to love you, accept you or approve of you, you are losing yourself in the other. To the extent that you fear rejection or judgment from another, you are losing yourself in the other. You are giving all your power to the other. If you feel loved or accepted, you feel good. If not, you collapse. Who has all the power? You have given it to others.

To awaken is to come back to yourself. It is to reclaim your power. It is time to free yourself from the need for love, approval and acceptance. Once again, you will have to go through a process of bringing to consciousness all the ways you lose yourself in others, and then very gently disengage from those patterns.

Question (female): It seems rather extreme to say that we lose ourselves in love.

Leonard's Answer: If you love someone, it is because you are love. That is all it means. If I am present and looking at you, then love is looking at you. If you are present looking at a tree or flower, then love is looking at the tree or flower. If you are present, then you are love. You are acceptance. You are compassion. It is a simple truth. If you need to be loved or accepted or prove yourself worthy, it just means that you have disconnected from the truth of who you really are. Most of us are desperate to be loved, because we feel unloved from childhood.

We are desperate to be accepted, because we feel that we are not good enough or not worthy. But looking for love and acceptance from others takes us further into the dream, and in the dream we are not loved, accepted or acknowledged.

The disciples of Jesus projected their love onto him and lost themselves in the process. They projected God onto him, and yet he tried to reflect to them that they are love and that God is within them. This pattern of projection has continued until the present day. When you are present, you are love and it matters not who or what you love.

In Presence, love is like the full moon on a cloudless night. It shines its light on all, without selection or discrimination.

Question (male): Is there a purpose to our lives?

Leonard's Answer: Yes, our true purpose in being here is to be here. It is that simple.

Male: I had a silent period in 1987. I remember it lasted for one minute.

Leonard: One minute. Well, you're due for your next minute of silence.

(Laughter)

Male: Good evening. Thank you again. I was here last night, and I came back because I wanted to see consistency.

Leonard: Was I consistent?

Male: Yes, actually. Your performance went across much better than I expected. It was very dramatic. I really got into it.

Leonard: Good.

Question (male): In the play, you are trying to take Jesus down from the cross. Can we also free Mary Magdalene from her reputation as a prostitute? And what was her relationship with Jesus?

Leonard's Answer: He loved her. But not in a way that he lost himself in her. They were together. She was his beloved. She was one of his closest disciples and more awake than any of the others.

Male: That's what I wanted to hear.

Question (female): I'm interested to hear what you think about the law of attraction.

Leonard: Are you referring to the book, *The Secret*?

Female: Yes.

Leonard's Answer: Sometimes the law of attraction is used by the ego in order to obtain more. If that is the case, it is an obstacle to awakening. One who is awake is not in need of more. One who is present is fulfilled by the present moment exactly as it is. From an awakened perspective, it is enough to know that the outer world manifests as a reflection of your inner world. If your inner world is the world of the mind, with all the emotional wounds and limiting beliefs based in your childhood, it will affect every aspect of your life.

For example, if you have a belief that you are not loved because you felt unloved as a child, you will attract into your life those who are unable to love. It does not matter how many affirmations you make and how positive your thoughts are. The deeper unconscious belief that you are not loved will prevail, until it is brought to consciousness in a way that leads to healing, completion and release.

On the other hand, if you have been through a process of healing and releasing the pain and limitations of the past and you are now fundamentally present, your interior world will be peaceful, calm, loving, accepting and full of gratitude and grace. What kind of outer world will manifest in response to that? If you truly recognize the abundance of the present moment, then abundance will flow into every aspect of your life.

Question (male): I really loved the play. I was wondering, did Jesus have an ego or did he live a life of service to others?

Leonard's Answer: Jesus had an ego, but it was a surrendered ego in service to him, just as he was in service to God. The surrender of his ego occurred in the desert, when he encountered what he thought was Satan or some kind of devil. Jesus had been fasting. He began to hallucinate and as a part of that hallucination, he projected his ego outside of him and it proceeded to tempt him.

Because it was projected outside of him, he could see and hear what it was up to and he could say no to its temptations. If it had not been projected outside of him, there would have been no distance between him and his ego and he could have been lost forever, a slave to his ego. Of course, Jesus thought it was Satan. Two thousand years would pass before Freud and Jung appeared on the earth to reveal the existence of the ego. Even though Jesus had never heard of the ego, he was able to resist its temptation and when Satan (his ego) realized that he could not be deceived, it surrendered.

However, most of us have been unable to resist the temptations of the ego. In order to open into mastery of your mind and ego, you will have to create a space between you and your ego. You can either fast for forty days and forty nights and hope to have the same hallucination as Jesus, or you can become very present. By becoming present you open up a space between you and your ego, and so you can be a witness to how it functions and how it pulls you out of Presence.

One of the great misunderstandings on the spiritual path is the belief that when we awaken, somehow the ego is eliminated. That is untrue and it is very unhelpful. Do you think the ego will stand idly by and allow itself to be annihilated? Even the slightest thought that you want to get rid of your ego will lock the ego in place. The ego thrives on the energy of judgment, rejection and struggle.

The only way to bring the ego to a place of relaxation and surrender is to awaken fully into Presence. When the ego encounters the energy of love, acceptance and compassion arising from within, it will begin to surrender. It won't happen all at once. It needs to know that it can depend upon you being present.

The ego will not surrender the reins of control if you're only present for a few minutes every now and then. But when you become established in Presence to such a degree that the ego cannot deceive you, then the ego will surrender.

Question (male): So, you are saying that Jesus was in service to God?

Leonard's Answer: Yes. He was in service to God and humanity. He was in service to God simply by being present at such a deep level that he experienced Oneness with God. Then God's Presence could flow through him. He was here to reveal the way of awakening and to demonstrate right relationship with God. He was surrendered to the will of God. But what does that mean? You cannot surrender to the will of God unless you are present. To surrender to the will of God simply means that you accept the present moment as it is and that you are responsive to the present moment.

Question (female): I really feel the call to Presence, but what do you suggest for someone who has a busy job which involves multi-tasking and all sorts of mental activity?

Leonard's Answer: If you need to think, then think. When there is no need to be thinking, then be present. If you are washing the dishes, having a shower or going for a walk, there is no need to be thinking. So be present. Be so deeply present that your mind is silent. And yet, one who is truly awake can think without disconnecting from Presence.

Awakening does not mean that we no longer think. It means that we no longer think unconsciously. We are no longer victims to a never-ending stream of unintended and unconscious thought. We consciously choose to think and when we have completed the thinking process, we return naturally to Presence and silence.

Being present does not interfere with our ability to think. It enhances it. The mind is an instrument of expression. When the mind is no longer cluttered with past emotions, limiting beliefs and anxiety about the future, it is a much clearer instrument of expression.

Question (female): Thank you. I have another quick question. Is there an antidote for losing ourselves in others?

Leonard's Answer: The only antidote is Presence. Nothing else will free you. From Presence, you can begin the process of bringing conscious awareness to how you lose yourself in others. Each time you notice that you are seeking love, approval or acceptance from another, just notice it. Acknowledge it to yourself and then gently disengage from it. It is just an old habit that will gradually subside as you bring it to consciousness without judgment.

Female: Thank you.

Leonard: You're welcome.

Question (female): In your book, you describe your awakening experiences. Are you anticipating another one of those experiences?

Leonard's Answer: I am not anticipating anything. I'm perfectly happy with the moment as it is. I'm not looking for more. This moment is enough. That's really an important statement. It is a realization that everyone must come to. The ego is constantly wanting more. It will never settle for the moment as it is, and it will very subtly drive you into the next moment looking for more. It is really a trick of the ego to prevent you from settling into Presence. Most people on a spiritual path are looking for a peak experience. They are looking for bliss. They are looking for the extraordinary. But often the present moment is ordinary. If you accept the present moment as ordinary, it will eventually reveal the present moment as extraordinary.

Question (male): Why would we choose the present moment if it is ordinary?

Leonard's Answer: The only reason you choose to be present is because the present moment is the truth of life, and you would rather be in the truth of life than lost in the illusory world of the mind. If you accept the present moment as ordinary, then you can settle there. You can deepen into Presence and then you will begin to feel the fullness of the moment. You will begin to feel peace and silence. You will experience a subtle sense of Oneness. You will feel whole and complete within yourself. And if you are present and overflowing with love, generosity and gratitude, then the extraordinary nature of Presence might open for you. If you approach the present moment in the right way, it will reveal its hidden treasures. And it will be far more beautiful than anything you can imagine with your mind.

Question (male): That sounds wonderful! How can I come to that place of fullness?

Leonard's Answer: Bring yourself fully present with this flower. It is very simple.

Just be here as the flower is here. Good! That's it. Just relax. Stay present with the flower.

(The audience member settles into Presence)

Now God has a question for you, "Beloved, is this moment enough, just as it is?"

Female: Yes!

Leonard: "Good, then you may stay," says God. Had you answered no, God would have replied, "No problem. Off you go in search of more. And good luck!"

Question (male): What is your concept of God?

Leonard's Answer: I have no concept of God. If I had a concept of God, it would be illusory, but let me share with you how I speak of God to others. I am not speaking to your mind. If you hear me with your mind, you will not know what I am speaking of. But if you are silent and present as I speak, my words will be perfectly clear and will reveal a truth that can only be known in silence.

For me it's so simple. God is the One in the all. God is the Silent Presence at the very heart of all things present. God is pure consciousness. God is the source from which everything arises and into which everything returns. God exists eternally as eternal Is-ness. God is this moment revealed. God is real, God is here now but we are not! If we want to experience the living Presence of God, we will have to come to where God is. We will have to become present. As we deepen into Presence, the mind will fall silent and we will begin to open into Oneness and feel and sense the living Presence of God in all things present. At times, it will be very subtle. At other times it will be overwhelming and unmistakable.

Now, do you have to call it God? No, not really but as a child,

I wasn't contaminated by religious concepts about God. I somehow escaped religious indoctrination. So, when I had my first awakening and opened so powerfully into Oneness and the eternal, I could feel and sense and see the Presence of God in everything so strongly that it seemed perfectly obvious to me that it was God. It was not God of the bible. It was not a religious God. It was not a God to believe in.

It was a direct experience of God, and I experienced God as overwhelmingly loving, accepting and allowing. I experienced God as an eternal silent Presence at the very heart of all things present. That Presence is always here. It is here right now. In this moment, you are all full of light. It is as if the room and everything and everyone in it is disappearing into light. It reminds me of that sentence from the bible, "When two or more are gathered together in my name, there I AM in the midst of them."

Question (female): I was wondering how you wrote and produced this play when everything you experienced was in the present moment. You must have used your mind to write the play.

Leonard's Answer: Being present does not eliminate your ability to think and use your mind. In the process of awakening, you have released many of the limiting beliefs, repressed emotions and judgments of yourself and others. You are no longer anxious about the future. As a result, your mind becomes clearer. You think more clearly and effectively. You don't get lost in that world of endless thought. You know that it is illusory in nature and you always have two feet planted in the present moment, even as you play in the world of time. You can think whenever it is appropriate to think, but now when you think, your thoughts are conscious and intentional and when you have finished thinking you naturally return to Presence.

Question (female): I listen to your audios a lot, especially when I'm driving. However, most of the time, my mind is very active. I try to be present in the way you suggest, but my thoughts persist. They never really stop. I'm wondering is there something further I can do?

Leonard's Answer: There are a number of reasons why your mind will not calm down and allow you to be present. The first is that the whole of humanity is habituated to living and functioning from within the mind. We have lived this way for many lifetimes. In addition to that, the whole of humanity has become addicted to thinking at such a deep level that we cannot stop thinking. Most of the time our thoughts are arising of their own accord and at an unconscious level. We are not even aware of the thoughts as they arise. Nevertheless, these unconscious thoughts, including all the limiting beliefs programmed into your mind, affect every aspect of life. If you want to slow the thoughts down and become more present, you will have to make being present the first priority in your life. You will have to become more and more aware of your thoughts as they arise and gently disengage from them.

But there are even more significant obstacles to calming the mind. If you become involved in judgment, you cannot free yourself. Judgment more than any other energy will keep you in the prison that is the world of the mind. And there is a powerful prison warden. It is your own ego, which has no intention of releasing you into the present moment. In fact, the resistance of the ego is the primary obstacle to human awakening.

Question (male): Could you say more about the resistance of the ego and how to overcome that resistance?

Leonard's Answer: As I said a moment ago, the ego's resistance is the primary obstacle to the awakening of consciousness. The whole of humanity is lost in a mind that never stops thinking. The ego won't allow the silence. It keeps us in a stream of never-ending thought that carries us into a remembered past or an imagined future and imprisons us there.

That is what the ego wants, and there are reasons for that.

The ego is the custodian of the separation. Its role is to protect you in a painful world of separation, where no one is truly present. This was very appropriate when you were a child. Your parents were not present in the way that you needed them to be. This gave rise to limiting beliefs and very difficult feelings like anger, hurt, need and fear. The feelings were too much to bear at such a young age and so the ego entered your life as your friend and protector. Its first role in your life was to help you to repress the painful and difficult feelings, so you would not have to feel them.

Its secondary role, which lasts the rest of your life, is to manage and control your life in a way that helps you to avoid those painful feelings, most of which arise around issues of isolation, worthiness, acceptance, inclusion and love.

But if you become present, you emerge from the dream. In the present moment, there is nothing to protect against. You are no longer seeking love or acceptance outside of yourself. You are no longer afraid of judgment or rejection. You are present even if no one else is. The ego's role as protector in a painful world of separation is rendered irrelevant, because you are no longer caught in the separation. As you awaken from the dream, the subtle feeling of separation is replaced by a subtle feeling of Oneness.

Because the ego is identified with its role, it will resist Presence and try to keep you in the past and the pain of separation. It has a bag of tricks to accomplish that. It keeps you in the past by generating thoughts and feelings involving blame, guilt, regret and resentment. As long as you identify with these thoughts, you will be held within the past. And the ego keeps you in the future with the promise of future fulfillment. As long as you believe that you can be fulfilled in the future, you will be subject to the ego's manipulations. Only the present moment can fulfill you. In order to free yourself, you will have to bring the temptations and manipulations of the ego into consciousness. You will have to get to know your own ego and you will have to come into right relationship with it.

This is only possible from Presence. A very clear space must open up between you and your ego. Otherwise, how can you witness what it is up to?

From Presence, you will have to reassure the ego that it has a continuing role in your life, even when you are fully present and awake. If you are to participate in the world of time, you need the ego. But in an awakened life, the ego's role is radically transformed. Its new role is to be of service to you within the world of time.

When the ego can trust that you are really present and it can depend on that, it will happily surrender its role as protector and take on its new role. It will no longer seek to pull you out of the present moment. When that happens, you are free.

When you awaken into Presence and come into right relationship with the ego, you will realize that the ego is your friend and protector, and that it has been waiting forever for the true master to arise from within. The true master is that dimension of you which is of this moment and only of this moment. It is the I AM Presence. It is the I AM that you are. But the ego has been waiting for so long that it has forgotten what it has been waiting for.

Question (female): What is your relationship to Judaism?

Leonard's Answer: I feel very close to Judaism, but not in a traditional or orthodox way. For me, the sole point in being Jewish is to fulfill the sacred covenant with God. To be delivered unto the Promised Land is to awaken in consciousness. The Promised Land is awakened consciousness, which reveals the sacred and the divine in everything. It reveals Oneness. It reveals Heaven on Earth. It has nothing to do with a physical location.

Jesus was a Jew. As he said, "I have not come to change the law, but to fulfill it." Jesus knew nothing of Christianity. Jesus was simply here to help Jews fulfill the covenant that began with Abraham.

Unfortunately, for the most part, both Jews and Christians missed the true meaning of his words. What would the world be like today if his message had been truly received and understood and humanity had awakened two thousand years ago? That was our opportunity then and we missed it. And now we are living with the consequences.

Question: Why are the Western religions so at odds with each other?

Leonard's Answer: I have a tremendous sense of the unfolding mystery that is woven into our existence. For me, it's as if God has planted a vine in the West and there are three branches of that vine: Judaism, Christianity and Islam.

Judaism has the goal, which is the coming together of man and God. It is deliverance from separation into Oneness. It is deliverance unto the Promised Land. It is the awakening of human consciousness into God consciousness. It is the coming together of the above and below, the formless and the world of form, the sacred and the mundane. This is reflected in the Star of David. The two triangles coming together represent a transcendence of duality into Oneness.

To fulfill their covenant with God, Jews will have to awaken into Presence at such a deep level that God is recognized as the silent Presence in all things present. Only then will Heaven on Earth be revealed as the Promised Land. Jesus was a Jew who represents the highest point in Jewish life. He was a fully awakened Being in One-ness with God. He experienced God in everything and God as everything. He was a revealer of the Way for the Jews. His words are powerful signposts, if not for those who were alive at the time, then surely for those who would follow.

If you try to interpret or understand his words with the mind, you will be led astray. He is speaking as a mystic. He is addressing "those with ears to hear." It is only when you are deeply present that the true meaning of his words is clear.

Mainstream and traditional Christianity developed as a result of a misunderstanding on the part of his disciples, and distortion and misrepresentation by those who came later and who were trying to attract followers. As Jesus says in the play, "How many would have been attracted to my teaching after my death, without myths and miracles to believe in?" Probably not many! This is not uncommon. Buddhists have done the same thing. They have woven a story around Buddha's enlightenment that is absolutely unnecessary and acts as an obstacle to awakening on the Buddhist path. Ultimately, awakening is normal. To be a fully realized Being is your natural state. It is unnatural to be lost in the mind, governed by our thoughts, opinions and beliefs.

Again, as Jesus says in the play, "Won't anyone choose to be present for no other reason than it is the truth of life?"

Then came Mohammed. He had his role to play in the flowering of the vine. The Jews have the goal. Jesus was a revealer of the Way. Mohammed shared with us how to live on this earth once we have found the Way and realized the goal. He taught us to live in total surrender to the will of God. But what does that mean?

To believe in God is a poor substitute for knowing God through your own direct experience. If you do not know God through your own direct experience, then without realizing it, you are surrendering and bowing to an illusory God, which takes you further and further into separation and illusion. To believe in God is a very poor substitute for knowing God and yet each of these religions is based in belief.

Because they are based in belief, these three religions have taken us into separation from each other and from God. The vine has split off from itself. The three branches have disconnected from the source. They are each equally lost in illusion.

If there is to be a full flowering of the vine, each of these religions will have to return to the source. They will have to transcend their separating beliefs and open into Presence and silence. They will have to recognize that there is only one God and they are of one vine. Christianity is an offshoot of Judaism, and Isaac and Ishmael are brothers. How difficult can it be to recognize their common roots?

When silence and the realization of Oneness is fully awakened within us, the religions will have to come into alignment with the truth. Either that, or they will disappear. As they come into alignment with the truth, they can continue with their spiritual traditions and rituals, but these will be transformed. The transformed rituals and traditions will be designed to bring us into Presence, Oneness and the direct experience of God.

There will be no more representatives of God and there will be a deep knowing that God exists within each one of us and is available to us whenever we are fully present. There will be a dissolving of all beliefs that keep us in separation.

Then, whenever a Jew, Christian or Muslim speaks of God, they will be speaking of the same God. They will no longer create God in their image, but rather surrender to the Oneness and mystery of God, a God that cannot be known with the mind.

When you open into the deepest level of silent Presence, you've transcended everything. You've transcended astrology, you've transcended karma, you've transcended understanding, you've transcended all your beliefs, you've transcended all relationships, all opinions, all concepts and all ideas. You've transcended religion. What is left? Just this moment as it is.

Now, very few people are willing to accept the present moment as it is. They're looking for the big bang. They want to be enlightened. They want bliss and ecstasy. But all of that is driven by the ego, which is never satisfied with the way things are and is always wanting more. To be truly awakened is actually very ordinary. It just means that you are here as the trees are here. You're here as the flowers are here. That's all it is. You're here, rather than lost in a world of not here. As you relax and deepen into the present moment, no matter how ordinary it appears to be, then slowly and gently the deeper levels of Presence will open up. The hidden treasures will be revealed. You can't hold on to anything. You can't seek anything. All you can do is relax into the present moment and accept the present moment as it is. Honor the present moment as the truth of life and the doorway to God, and it will reveal its hidden treasures.

Question (male): If our minds are silent when we are present, how can we function in the world without thought?

Leonard's Answer: That is a very important question. It is true that at the very deepest level of Presence, your mind is silent. You are fully immersed in the present moment. There is no past or future, because there is no thought. All sense of yourself as a separate individual has dissolved. You are fully immersed in the mystery. At this deep and profound level of Presence, you cannot participate in the world of time because there is no time. All you can do is relax and enjoy the bliss and serenity of the eternal Now. In Buddhist terminology, this would be a state of Samadhi.

But you do not always have to be at this profound depth of Presence. You can be lightly present. You are still present, but now the past and future are available to you. You can think, but you do not get lost in thought. You can remember the past and plan for the future, but you still remain fundamentally present. You can play in the dream, but you know it is a dream and you never go so far into it that you disconnect from Presence.

It is helpful to view Presence as existing on a vertical axis. You can move up and down on this vertical axis simply by becoming more or less finely attuned to the present moment. As you become more deeply present, there is a point on this vertical axis where you go beyond time. Beyond this point you open into Oneness, truth, love and God. You open into the mystery. You open into the realization of Heaven on Earth. Above this point on the vertical axis, you can live your life in a normal way, but you never completely disconnect from Presence and you can return to the deepest level of profound Presence instantly and without any effort.

Question (female): When we are present, do we need to be aware of our shadow?

Leonard's Answer: When you're present there is no shadow, but in order to become present, you will have to reveal the shadow. When you are fully present, you are in Oneness. In Oneness, there is joy without pain, love without hate or life without death.

In other words, in Presence you have transcended duality. You have transcended the past and future and now you are present.

When you are not present, you are in duality. In duality, there is past and future, joy and pain, happiness and sadness, life and death, and hope and despair. You will be governed by your past and all your limiting beliefs and repressed emotions, most of which originate in your childhood. Or you will create anxiety for yourself by getting too involved in future outcome. Most of us on a spiritual path seek the light and reject the darkness. But that is a form of judgment and all judgment throws us out of balance within duality.

We will have to learn to live in balance within the world of duality. We have to own, acknowledge and accept every aspect of ourselves without judgment. We have to accept both sides of duality. Only when duality is balanced within us will the doorway to Oneness be opened.

Question (female): I accept what you mean by the 'I Am Presence' but it is harder for me to accept the word God. What do you mean by God?

Leonard's Answer: First, I would say that God cannot be

known with the mind. God cannot be understood or defined. The best that the mind can do is believe in God. But to believe in God is a very poor substitute for knowing God through your own direct experience. And once you know, there is no need for belief.

For me, God is the silent Presence at the very heart of all things present. God is real. God is here now. But we are not. We have become absorbed into the past and future world of the mind. If you want to experience the living Presence of God in all things present, you will have to come to where God is. You will have to come out of the mind and become present. When we become fully present, we will begin to sense the Presence that is in everything. This Presence is what I mean by God, and it is reflected in the expression, "God is omnipresent."

When we believe in God, we are creating God in our image, whereas in truth we are created in the image of God. You cannot know God with the mind but you can experience God in those moments of deep Presence. You don't have to call it God, but if you don't want to call it God, it is because your mind was contaminated around that word when you were a child. Many people have told me that as children they had a strong sense of God but as they became indoctrinated by religion they lost their connection to God. Many of them finished up as agnostics or atheists and the rest pursued alternative spiritual paths in search of something beyond what religions have to offer.

If the word 'God' has been contaminated for you, I suggest you do some healing and clearing around that word. When you are present I could ask you, "Who is present in this moment?" The most perfect response to that question is simply, "I AM," but those words must be spoken from Presence and not from within the mind.

When Moses ascended Mt. Sinai and was asked by God to liberate his people from slavery in Egypt, Moses asked God, "Who shall I say has sent me?"

God's response was simple and clear. "Tell them, 'I am that I am' has sent you." As you become more and more present, the I AM Presence is revealed at the very center of your Being. It is at the very center of your Being that you open into Oneness with God.

Question (male): Do you feel that we are now more ready to be present than we were two thousand years ago?

Leonard's Answer: Yes, and I will tell you why. Because of our unconsciousness, we are so destructive that we are taking ourselves to the very edge. And as we get closer to the edge, we will have to respond to the truth or it's over for humanity. I've been sharing this teaching for over forty years now. In the early days, it was so hard to bring people out of the mind into Presence. I had to resort to all sorts of outrageous interventions to get them into Presence. Now, it is so much easier. I can walk into a room with over two hundred people in attendance. In less than a minute, most are quite deeply present. In fact, I can see quite a few in this audience tonight who are quite deeply present. Humanity is already in the process of awakening, but there are powerful forces of resistance, including our own egos.

Question (male): How did we all get so lost?

Leonard's Answer: It has a lot to do with our need to avoid physical and emotional pain. Somewhere in our past, probably many lifetimes ago, the pain that we were experiencing was too much to bear. I am speaking of pain caused by war, famine, disease, neglect, poverty and even torture. We have all had some very difficult past life incarnations. The only way that we could avoid the pain that we were experiencing in that moment of suffering was to leave that moment. But where would we go?

The only possibility was to enter the past and future world of the mind and seek escape there. We literally thought our way out of the present moment into a dream made up of past memories or future imaginings and now we are lost there. We cannot find our way back to the present moment. It was a valid decision at that time, but we forgot to come back. Our avoidance of pain is now a deep and habitual pattern that humanity is caught in. The great irony is that in this present moment there is no pain and there is nothing we need to avoid or escape from. The pain that we are avoiding is from the past, not the present. It is just an unconscious memory of the pain. Whether that memory is from a past life or from childhood, it does not really matter.

The real issue is that we are now habituated to living in the mind and we are addicted to thinking, which keeps us locked into the past or future and out of the present moment. There is no pain in this moment, but still we resist returning to Presence.

Question (male): Well, I just want to applaud the entire show and performance. I think it's absolutely brilliant and delighted that you've created it and I hope it goes far and wide. I wonder if there might be some openness within the non-fundamentalist Christian community where there is a certain spaciousness and receptivity. I'd love to see exposure to that.

Leonard's Answer: Well, let me tell you a secret.

Male: Sure.

Leonard: The day after this finishes here, which is next Sunday, I fly to Kansas City to perform the play before a really large Unity Church audience. The only question for me is will it be too much for them? I don't know yet, we'll see.

Male: I just think it's absolutely wonderful and I hope it really is received well and makes a difference.

Leonard: Can I tell you another secret?

Male: Sure.

Leonard: I wrote the play for you.

(*Laughter*)

Male: I know you did. That's why I came.

(*Laughter*)

Leonard: And everyone else who's able to respond. It's that simple.

Question (male): As we become more present, does that flow onto others? Does it affect others?

Leonard's Answer: Absolutely yes. Our only real hope is that enough of us awaken and settle into the deep, silent Presence that I'm speaking of. If enough of us awaken, it will affect the collective. If we can reach a critical mass of awakened Beings on this planet, then suddenly the whole of humanity will awaken, without any effort on their part.

Each moment that you are truly present it is like dropping a tiny pebble of light into a vast pool of human unconsciousness. Ripples of light!

Question (female): I would like you to talk a little bit about the role of gratitude in the context of awakening.

Leonard's Answer: God responds to generosity and gratitude more than anything else. It's as simple as that and the more you are present, the more grateful you will feel. Now, it's really hard to fabricate gratitude. Gratitude has to be utterly authentic, arising from Presence. For many people, the only way to open into gratitude is to own, acknowledge and confess their lack of gratitude, not as a judgment but as a part of the process of healing and awakening.

Question (male): Hello Leonard.

Leonard: Hi. Is that Pedro?

Male: Yes sir.

Leonard: Hi Pedro.

Male: Can you speak a little about reacting and responding?

Leonard's Answer: Yes. Well, the meaning is really hidden within the words. React means I am re-enacting something from my past, which I am now projecting onto the present moment. My experience of the present moment is distorted by my projections.

To respond is quite different. You respond to whatever is happening in the moment. The past is not involved. You are present, calm and you respond. There is nothing from the past influencing your response. When you are present, your response is always appropriate because it is not distorted by projections from the past. However, before you can get to a state of consciousness where you respond rather than react, you will have to go through a process of liberating the limiting beliefs and repressed emotions from the past so that they no longer project onto the present.

Question (male): Do we have free will and if so, how does that relate to the will of God?

Leonard's Answer: We have free will and there is a simple reason for that. God has free will, and because we are created in the image of God, we must also have free will. This means that every hour of every day, we are free to make our own choices and those choices determine our experience of life. For the most part, we don't realize that consequences inevitably flow from the choices we make.

If you choose to eat unhealthy food or if you choose to drink that extra glass of wine or beer and then drive, there are consequences.

However, most of us made choices in our childhood which are still impacting our lives today and which are affecting us at an unconscious level. For example, many of us made an unconscious choice in childhood to repress painful and difficult feelings. At that time, it was an appropriate choice because the feelings were too much for a young child to bear. But that choice to repress your feelings is still functioning at an unconscious level within you.

Many of us chose to close our hearts to love, because of a fear of being hurt. But as a consequence of that unconscious childhood choice, we live without love in our lives. These childhood choices are affecting every aspect of our lives and relationships.

Until we bring these unconscious choices to consciousness, there is no way to modify or change them. Perhaps it is time to review your choices. Perhaps it is time to allow all the repressed emotions to surface into conscious and responsible expression. Perhaps it is time to open your heart and experience a level of love that you have never experienced before. Perhaps it is time to choose a life without judgment, blame, guilt and expectation. By reviewing and changing your choices, you change your life.

But there is a much deeper choice that you will have to make if you are to liberate yourself from the dream and open into Presence and Oneness. It is a fundamental choice at the very heart of free will. This fundamental choice will not only affect your experience of life, but it will change how humanity lives upon this beautiful planet.

Now this is God speaking!

"Beloveds, which world do you choose to live in? Do you choose the present moment, the truth of life, where I am the Creator? Or do you choose the world of your mind, a world of separation and illusion, but there you get to be the creator? Which world do you choose?"

It is as if God gave us free will and is waiting patiently for those who will voluntarily surrender it.

I am reminded of the Lord's prayer. "Thy will be done on Earth as it is in Heaven."

But how do we surrender to the will of God? There is only one way. The first step is to become present. Then, when you are present, be responsive to whatever is occurring within the moment of now. If it is happening now, then it must be the will of God. So be responsive and not reactive to whatever is happening now.

The only thing God wants of us is that we are truly present and responsive. Then we will open to an entirely new and awakened dimension of life based in love, acceptance, compassion, wisdom and the realization of God and Oneness.

Question (male): But how can you say that war, famine, cruelty and abuse that is happening in our world is the will of God?

Leonard's Answer: It is not the will of God. As I said, we have been given free will. These things are a direct result of human unconsciousness. When we are caught within the mind we are living in a state of separation, and the feeling of being separate drives us towards all sorts of destructive behavior. There is so much fear, greed, judgment and lust for power in our world because we are lost in the illusion of separation.

There is no recognition of Oneness. But the moment we settle into Presence, we come out of our separate worlds. We come into the one world revealed through the doorway of the present moment. Everything will change as we become present and begin to open into Oneness. Then you might just realize that I am you, posing as me.

Male: Thank you.

Question (male): Hi Leonard, my name is Paul and I guess I haven't really experienced this Presence that you speak of.

Leonard: You haven't?

Male: I have not and I was hoping you could guide me into it.

Leonard's Answer: Sure. I share a very simple key to being present, which is actually revealed in the play as well. It's so simple. When you're in the mind, you're somewhere in the past or future. Thoughts are always of the past or future, so whenever you think you take yourself into the mind.

Now, in order for you to come out of the past and future world of the mind into the present moment, you just bring yourself present with something that's here in the moment with you. If you can see it, hear it, feel it, taste it, touch it or smell it in this moment, you can be present with it. And the moment you are present in this way, you will come out of the mind. Thoughts will stop without you trying to stop them.

So now, close your eyes and be very present with your body as it breathes. Be present with the sound you hear, moment to moment. Be present and conscious in the movement of your body. Be present with the feeling of your feet touching the floor. Be present with the feeling of the chair against your back. It really is as simple as being present with whatever is in the present moment with you.

Any moment that you are truly present, you are an awakened Being. But you are not limited to being present with your eyes closed. Open your eyes now and be present with the flower in front of you. The flower is here. You are here. You are sharing this moment of Presence with the flower. You can even speak to the flower.

"I am here now. I am often lost in my story, but I am here now. Thank you for being present with me."

You can share with the flower how you are feeling right now.

"Flower, in this moment of Presence with you, I am experiencing peace and silence. I am experiencing love. I am experiencing your beauty."

The flower has been waiting for a long time to hear those words. It will open up even more for you and it will take you into deeper levels of Presence. If you remember to be present many times each day, then the awakened state of Presence will slowly and gradually open up within you.

Now that is only half of the picture. You will discover that being present is remarkably simple. What is more difficult is remaining present as we live our lives, go to work and participate in our relationships. It is so easy to be pulled back into the mind.

That is why there are two steps to this teaching. The first step is learning the art of being present. But the second step involves bringing conscious awareness to all the ways you are pulled out of Presence. What are the obstacles to being present? What is still unconscious, unhealed and unresolved within you from your past? What is holding you in the dream? Step one of this teaching leads to Presence. Step two leads to mastery of your mind and ego. Both steps are essential for true awakening.

Question (female): What do you mean by the dream, the story?

Leonard's Answer: If you are not present, then you are in your story. If you are thinking, you are in your story. If you are in the past or future, you are in your story. Everything outside of this moment is your story. You are in a world of memory and imagination.

You are in a world of concept, opinion and belief. You are not here now. Sometimes I refer to it as the world of your mind. Sometimes I refer to it as your story. Sometimes I refer to it as your dream, but it is all the same thing.

I am not saying that the story should go away or that you should not use your mind. That would be ridiculous. Without thought and the world of the mind, you could not participate in the world of time. Without the mind, there is no time. You could not go to work. You could not plan for the future. You could not remember the past. You could not function in the normal sense of the word. So, keep your story. Enjoy your life in the world of time. Use your mind. Just do not believe in any of it. And don't venture so far into the dream that you disconnect from Presence.

Question (female): I am not sure I understand. Are you saying that the dream occurs within the mind?

Leonard's Answer: Think of the mind as a very limited level of consciousness. It is a field of consciousness that you enter into whenever you think. It is quite literally a field of dreams. It is within this field that the dream appears.

But the dream is not real. It is made up of thought, memory, imagination, idea, concept, opinion and belief. You are dreaming of things that are not of the present moment. It is a kind of fantasy generated within the mind and mostly, the dream is self-generating. And the dream is not limited to when you are asleep in your bed. You open your eyes in the morning, you get out of bed, you have breakfast, then you go to work. You think you are awake, but you are not. You are still dreaming in the sense that past memory or future imagining is still occurring within you and it is distorting your sense of reality. You are projecting the dream onto the present moment. The dream contains within it all the limiting beliefs, repressed feelings, fears and judgments that keep you in the past. It contains all your hopes, dreams and desires that take you into the future.

When you become present, you are opening into an entirely new and awakened level of consciousness. Now you are in a field of Presence. A field of truth. A field of peace, love and compassion. A field of Oneness. Everything within this field of Presence is of the present moment. Everything you see, hear, feel, taste, touch or smell exists within the present moment and within this field of Presence. In one sense, you are this field of Presence, and everything you experience within this field is occurring within you. There is no sense of separation as you open into Oneness. There is no judgment. There is no past or future.

Perhaps we could take it one step further and call it the field of God. Now you are awake in God consciousness and at the deeper levels of Presence, the field of God reveals Heaven on Earth. Come, join me in this field! There are flowers everywhere.

Question (female): I ended up with the mic, so I guess I have a question.

Leonard: OK.

Question (female): How do you deal with people who have no interest in becoming present and are resistant to any kind of change? Do you try and persuade them?

Leonard's Answer: Two thousand years ago, Jesus said that his message was for those with ears to hear and for those with eyes to see. He knew that not everyone was ready for the truth. He was seeking those who could respond to his Presence and his words, and he would know them by their response. Those who could not or would not respond, he referred to them as dead. The majority of people at that time were caught within the mind and governed by their ego. Most were unable to respond to truth even if it was clearly presented to them.

Another reason that they could not respond has to do with the nature of truth. "Truth cannot and will not penetrate into the world of belief. Belief must surrender of its own accord before the truth will enter."

Many people have firm and rigid beliefs. They are unwilling to have their cherished beliefs questioned and so there is little chance of them responding to the truth.

I am not a proselytizer. I am not trying to convince or persuade anyone. If anyone is genuinely interested in this teaching, they will find their way to me or I will find my way to them. It is really quite mysterious how we find each other in this way. I don't share this teaching, even with my friends, unless there is an invitation for me to do so.

Question (female): That leads me to my second question. I'm actually studying psychology right now with the desire to go into the field of psychology. What would you say about that?

Leonard's Answer: Well, as far as I'm concerned you are a free Being and you can do whatever you feel drawn to. The problem is that much of what we pursue and get involved in can actually be an obstacle to our awakening. For example, the study of psychology can fill your mind with theory, concepts and methodologies that take you further into the mind. You become identified with what you have learned and then it becomes more difficult to let it all go. To truly awaken, we really have to surrender everything at the level of mind.

If you feel drawn to be a psychologist that is fine, but always know that there is a deeper level of truth that transcends all psychological concepts, beliefs and methodologies. If you are to awaken in this lifetime, then being present has to be your first priority. If you do awaken into Presence, then your practice as a psychologist will be greatly enhanced. It will give you a level of insight that most psychologists don't have.

We are all living in a world where no one is present. This leads to a very subtle and mostly unconscious feeling that we are alone and separate. So much of our lives are devoted to avoiding the pain of feeling separate. Most people are living with fear, limiting beliefs, repressed feelings and judgments of themselves and others.

If, as a psychologist, you can be present with your clients and intervene from a place of Presence, that will be profoundly healing. When people are living mostly from within their minds, they are caught in a story, a dream. Instead of trying to fix their story or their dream, it is much more effective to help them to wake up out of the dream. Then they will discover that there is nothing wrong with them and that there is nothing to fix.

Female: It's a good thing I didn't finish my application to that master's program.

(*Laughter*)

Question (male): Is psychology sometimes effective?

Leonard's Answer: Of course, it can be very helpful. There are many people on this planet who could care less about awakening or being present. They relate much more to a psychological approach to healing. Or they see a therapist hoping to be able to fix themselves. They don't realize that the true solution is in awakening, not in psychology. But it doesn't mean psychology doesn't have its place and can't be helpful. Just talking to a psychologist or counselor who is empathic and compassionate can be very healing. However, to awaken to the deeper and more mystical levels of Presence, psychology will have to be released. Philosophy will have to be released. Religion and spiritual practice will have to be released. You can come back to these things, but in order to awaken you will have to let it all go. At least for now!

By letting it all go, you create an opening for Presence to awaken more fully within you. Then you can return to your practice as a psychologist or a therapist, but now you will be present in your interaction with your clients. This will be much more effective. Your focus will not be on fixing the dream but rather guiding your clients to awaken from the dream.

Question (male): How will I know when I am present?

Leonard's Answer: One of the keys to awakening is to know the distinction between when you are truly present and when you are in the mind. There is a clear and simple test. When you are fully present, your mind is silent and you are very present with whatever is here in the moment with you. You are nowhere else.

The only way you can be somewhere else is to think your way out of the present moment. And where will you go? There is only one place you can go if you are not present and that is the world of your mind, the dream, the story. The problem is that we cannot stop thinking. We are addicted to thinking and so the thoughts just keep on coming.

It is important not to reject or judge the thoughts. Just notice when you are thinking and gently return to Presence. Slowly but surely the mind will relax and the thoughts will slow down. It is important not to be in a hurry. Just notice when you are thinking and gently return to Presence. Sooner or later, you will notice how much quieter your mind is and every now and then, you will find yourself at the deepest levels of silence and peace. You will feel whole and complete in this moment. You will feel peaceful, generous and grateful. And you will have a sense of Oneness and wonder as you open into the mystery of timeless existence.

Question (female): Thank you first for your beautiful performance.

Leonard: Thank you.

Question (female): You used the word 'ego' several times in the play. Can you say more about the ego's role in our lives?

Leonard's Answer: If you are to awaken, you must have answers to certain questions regarding the ego. What is the ego? What is its role in your life? How does it function? Why does it resist you becoming present and how can you overcome that resistance?

The ego is not the enemy. It's actually your friend and protector in a world where no one is present. It came into your life when you were very young. It was aware of the limiting beliefs developing within you as a result of your parent's inability to be present with you.

These limiting beliefs include:
- I am alone, I'm separate
- I'm abandoned
- There is no one really here for me
- I am not loved
- I am not accepted
- I am not good enough
- I can't do it
- I'm a failure
- It is not OK to feel and express my feelings
- It is not OK to ask for what I want
- I can't have what I want
- I have to do what they want
- I have to be good
- I have to do the right thing
- I am not worthy
- I don't want to be here
- There must be something wrong with me
- I don't count
- I don't fit in, I don't belong

Can you imagine how these limiting beliefs have affected your life and relationships?

In addition to these limiting beliefs, you had to deal with painful and difficult feelings associated with the limiting beliefs. The ego's role is to help you manage these limiting beliefs and difficult feelings. The first thing it does is help you to repress the painful feelings so that you won't have to feel them. Then it assumes a management role, more or less taking over your life. It develops strategies to help avoid a repetition of the hurt and pain you experienced in your childhood and it is trying to bring into your life what it thinks you need.

For example, if one of those limiting beliefs is that you are not loved, the ego will develop strategies designed to get you the love that you need. But even if many people are loving you in this moment, you won't feel it. You won't let it in, because at a deeper level you believe that you are not loved. If you have the belief that you are not good enough, the ego will develop strategies designed to prove to others that you are good enough. But nothing really works. Even if you become very successful, you will still feel that you are not good enough, because of that limiting belief.

The problem with the ego is that it has to keep you in that painful past to justify its role as your protector. In other words, it has been protecting you from pain that occurred in the past, mostly in your childhood. If you become present, there is no pain. This removes the ego's reason for existing. It does not want to be rendered irrelevant. And so, it will resist you opening into Presence and it is very skillful at pulling you out of the present moment.

So how do we overcome the resistance of the ego? You cannot defeat the ego. Any attempt to defeat the ego would simply be the ego trying to defeat itself. It won't work. The only thing that will actually bring the ego to a place of surrender is the energy of love, acceptance and compassion. There cannot be any hint of judgment or rejection of the ego. You will have to come into right relationship with the ego and that is only possible when you are present. When you are present, you are love, acceptance and compassion. You are without judgment. Only when you are present can you come into right relationship with the ego so that the ego will gradually and gently ease its resistance to Presence. There is so much more I can tell you about the ego, but I am limited by the tyranny of time.

Question (male): Your teachings, and I consider this play to be a form of teaching, seem to be very consistent with the Vedanta philosophy that emerged out of India. I'd be interested to know how much of your teaching is based on the study of Vedanta, either through the intellect or through practical experience. What tools or what practical exercises did you use to support your awakening?

Leonard's Answer: I have been told that what I teach is quite close to Vedanta spirituality or philosophy, but I have not read any books on Vedanta, nor have I been exposed to it, other than in a fairly superficial way. Like Vedanta, this is a teaching that is intended to lead us out of duality into Oneness and Is-ness. In fact, everything I share is informed by the series of awakenings that I have experienced in my life. My sense of it is that the closer we come to the truth, the more it's going to sound the same, no matter who is speaking.

Perhaps at the end of our journey of awakening, we will just be silent. We'll find ourselves beyond words, beyond concepts, beyond ideas, beyond spiritual practice, beyond understanding, even beyond the notion of enlightenment. We will simply be immersed in the moment of Now, experiencing the Is-ness of existence.

Question (male): There seems to be a lot of talk these days about being in the Now. I think it began in the sixties with some authors like Ram Dass and J. Krishnamurti. In the play, you said that if you can be in the Now, you can experience God or God consciousness. How does one transcend the mind and become present enough that you experience God?

Leonard's Answer: First of all, you have to let go of the desire for bliss, ecstasy or enlightenment. You even have to let go of the desire for God. There cannot be any sense of an outcome, because that will keep you in the future and you will not find God in the future. You will only find God in the present moment. So just focus on being present and what you will experience will depend on how deeply present you are. It will also depend on what you bring to the present moment. If you are deeply present and overflowing with love, gratitude and generosity, the present moment will respond to you and begin to reveal its hidden treasures. Everything in physical form is the body of God. Bring yourself present with the body of God and you will begin to feel and sense the Presence of God in all things present.

Question (male): A lot of people are saying that we're currently in a transition to a higher level of consciousness. It seems to me that we're moving into a time when human beings will be co-creators with God in the evolution of this planet. Can you comment on this?

Leonard's Answer: I love your optimism and it is true. The awakening of consciousness is available to us now more than at any time in human history. But as Jesus said, it is only for those with ears to hear. There are so many people on this planet who adhere rigidly to the old way of living on this planet. Some might even react violently to any kind of change or to anything that challenges their beliefs.

At a personal level, most of us will not even consider the possibility of awakening until the dream becomes so full of pain and suffering that there is no choice. Will this be how it unfolds at the collective level? Will we take ourselves so close to the edge that we either awaken or perish? How many are ready for awakening? If you are to awaken, you will have to give up believing in your thoughts, opinions, concepts and beliefs. You will have to own, acknowledge and confess every aspect of who you have become in the dream. You will have to bring the limiting beliefs to conscious awareness. You will have to liberate the feelings from the past repressed within you.

You will have to come into right relationship with your ego. You will have to transcend judgment in your life. You will have to take responsibility for yourself at every level. And first, you will have to learn the art of being present.

If people knew the rewards that await them in Presence, they would not hesitate. Those rewards include peace, joy, love, silence, Oneness, God and Heaven on Earth. But the most beautiful thing about being present is that you are dwelling in the truth of life instead of being lost in a world of illusion.

Question (male): Yes, I've been there in that place that you're talking about and in that place everything is perfect. There's nothing to be done. I have one question though. When I come back from that state of Presence and Oneness, I'm almost depressed. What is there for me to do now?

Leonard's Answer: You just said that you have had these wonderful deep moments of Presence and peace where everything is perfect, right? And then, when you come back, you are almost depressed. But where do you come back to? You come back into the world of the mind and ego. You come back into the past and future. You come back into the story, the dream. You come back into a world of separation and illusion.

It is as if God gave you a taste of Heaven on Earth. God wanted you to know the truth of who you are, the truth of life, the truth of love and the truth of God. But then God dropped you back into the soup of human unconsciousness. God dropped you back into your dream. Now why would God do that? The answer is simple. God wants you to awaken into Presence and Oneness, but God also wants you to be a master of your mind and ego. The only way that you can arise in mastery of your mind and ego is to take the fall. What is the fall? It is the shift from awakened Presence to the world of the mind and the truth is that the whole of humanity is fallen.

But instead of seeing it as a failure or a problem, you can see it as an opportunity. Each time you are pulled back into the dream or you find yourself caught within the dream, you have an opportunity to witness how that happened. You have an opportunity to recognize what is incomplete or unhealed within you.

If you are to become a master of your mind and ego, you will have to find answers to the following questions:

How do you get pulled out of Presence involuntarily? What are the hooks in you that enable you to be pulled out of Presence? What are the limiting beliefs still affecting you at an unconscious level? Which repressed feeling has been triggered? How do you lose yourself in others? Are you judging yourself or others? How do you keep yourself in the dream? How does the ego manage to pull you out of Presence? Why does the ego resist Presence? What do you need to let go of to come out of the dream and return to Presence?

As you arise in mastery of your mind and ego, you will find yourself settling into Presence. You will discover that you can play in the world of time without disconnecting from Presence.

As you become more and more present, first you will experience Oneness, then you will experience God and then you will experience Heaven on Earth. On the other hand, if you go too far into the world of the mind and you become lost there, it will eventually lead you into a kind of hell on Earth. Heaven and hell exist here on Earth in this very moment. It all depends on your level of consciousness and the degree to which you have awakened into Presence. It's really incredibly worthwhile to awaken in this lifetime and it's available to everyone, as long as you know the Way. But what I am sharing is only "for those with ears to hear."

If you want to hold on rigidly to your beliefs, opinions and to the way of living that you are familiar with, then you will not awaken.

Question (female): I'm puzzled when I meet people that have practiced meditation for many years and yet they still seem to have a lot of ego. I could say the same about some spiritual teachers that I have met.

Leonard's Answer: For most people on a spiritual path, the ego can become very involved in meditation or other kinds of spiritual practice. With any kind of practice there's always a future agenda. You might devote yourself to various practices hoping for some future outcome. That is a built-in obstacle to awakening. You cannot awaken at some time in the future. You can only awaken now. The good news is that Now is always re-presenting itself to you, inviting you to be present. But most of us ignore the invitation. We are too busy with our meditations, spiritual practices and our quest for enlightenment to respond to the invitation.

There is much we have to learn about the ego if we are to awaken. What is the ego? What is its role in your life? How does it function? Why does it resist you becoming present? How does it pull you out of the present moment? How can you overcome the resistance of the ego?

The truth is that no one can defeat the ego. Not Buddha, not Jesus, not anyone. Any intention to defeat or get rid of the ego is coming from the ego itself. It is just a trick to keep you in its world of the mind, where it is in control. If you cannot defeat the ego, then how can you overcome its resistance. The answer is clear and simple. You will have to come into right relationship with the ego and right relationship with the ego is only possible from Presence. When you are present, you are without judgment. You are the energy of love, acceptance and compassion. You are allowing. This is the energy you bring to the ego.

As you come into right relationship with the ego, it will gradually surrender the reigns of control. It won't disappear, but its role in your life will be radically and profoundly changed.

Male: Hi Leonard. This is my first experience with you and it's uncanny because I am a student of A Course in Miracles. And a lot of what you are sharing here is very aligned with A Course in Miracles.

Leonard's Answer: I've never read A Course in Miracles.

Male: Well, it's uncanny.

Leonard: I'm not sure if this is true or not, because I haven't read it, but I have been told that A Course in Miracles regards this physical world as illusory, somehow a projection of our minds.

Male: Which is exactly what you're saying.

Leonard: No, it's not! It's far from what I'm saying. The distinction is clear. The world of illusion is everything outside of this moment. It exists within your mind as memory, imagination, concepts, ideas, beliefs, opinions and a continuing stream of thoughts, most of which arise at an unconscious level. All of that is illusory. We are creating it with our thoughts and within our minds. But it is not real. When you awaken, you will discover that it was all a dream.

Then what is real? Whatever is in the present moment with you is real. If you can see it, hear it, feel it, taste it, touch it or smell it in this moment, then it is of the present moment. You are not imagining it. You are not remembering it. It is of the present moment and so it is real. If you shift your focus and become present with something that is in the present moment with you, then you will come out of the mind. Thoughts will stop without you trying to stop the thoughts. Without thought, you will encounter the truth and reality of the present moment, free of your projections from the past onto the present. However, there is another reason why I differ from A Course in Miracles. There is no way to leave the illusory world of the mind oth-er than by becoming present with what is here in the moment with you. If whatever is in the present moment is also illusory, then we will simply be moving from one state of illusion to another. But that is not my experience. By becoming present, we transcend the world of the mind. We are opening into another dimension of our existence, an awakened dimension, free of the dream and free of our projections. The confusion arises because the energy body exists within the physical body. Whatever is in physical form also exists as energy. As you become more deeply present, you might penetrate beyond the physical body into the energy body. Then it is likely that whatever you are present with will begin to dissolve into light.

This is even more likely if you are present with another human Being who is also deeply present. Then all sorts of interesting things can arise. To tune into the energy body is not a denial of the physical body. It is inclusive of the physical body and at the same time, it is transcendent of the physical body. So just relax. Be present with what is here now. At first you will be present with the physical body, then you will open into the energy body, then you will open into Oneness, then you will become aware of the Presence of God in all things present and then Heaven on Earth will be revealed. Beyond that there is infinite and eternal silence. Pure consciousness. Nothing-ness, like a vast black hole waiting eternally for you to find your way to it.

Question (female): When you experienced your first moments in Presence, did those moments turn into minutes and then hours and then days? Sometimes I have had eight minutes in Presence and sometimes I have had entire days in Presence.

Leonard: Entire days, that's pretty damn good. To answer your question, it didn't happen gradually for me from moments to minutes to days to months. I had a huge explosion into Presence. It was completely beyond my control and it felt like I was in many different dimensions at the same time. Time completely disappeared. It lasted for about three months at this level of intensity and then it began to settle, and I was able to function in the world once again. For most people, I do not recommend a sudden awakening. A much easier way is a gentle awakening, where you gradually become more present and you gradually arise in mastery of your mind and ego.

Whether you experience a sudden awakening or a gradual awakening, we all finish up in the same place, which is here now. And you know, we don't have to be deeply present all the time. It's OK to play in the world of time. Just don't get lost there. You have to be able to flow freely between the timeless world of Now and the world of time. But you are sufficiently grounded in Presence that you no longer get caught in the story.

Question (male): Thinking about one of the more extreme examples of unconsciousness, what kind of spiritual perspective do you take in dealing with the minds of Muslim extremists? And, how do you bring in the concept of turning the other cheek in addressing this global issue?

Leonard's Answer: Muslim extremists are a perfect example of people who have gone so far into the world of illusion that the only way that they can maintain themselves in that illusory world is to become more and more rigid in their beliefs. The more rigidly we hold to our beliefs, the more dangerous we are to each other and the natural world. We can justify any act of abuse or cruelty in the name of our beliefs.

History is overflowing with examples of war waged in the name of our beliefs. If you believe that all non-Muslims are infidels, and if you believe that by killing the infidels you will go to Heaven and that in Heaven you will have your pick of seven naked virgins, then you just might be willing to blow yourself up as a way of killing the infidels. It is so insane. The same rigidity of belief exists in all the religions, although not all religions are engaged in such a level of violence.

Question (male): Hi, can you guide me into the experience of being in the present?

Leonard's Answer: There's a very simple key to being present. Just bring yourself present with something that's here in the moment with you. If you can see it, hear it, feel it, taste it, touch it or smell it in this moment, you can be present with it. That's it. It's so simple. So just for a moment, bring yourself present with any one of these flowers. Have the sense that you're bringing the gift of your Presence to the flower. Just be here with it. Be here as the flower is here. That's all it is. If you're really present, you'll notice your thoughts have stopped and your mind is silent. You will feel a deep sense of peace.

Now, take a moment to slowly look around the room. Notice how much there is for you to be present with. You can be present with what you see. You can be present with the sound you hear in this moment. You can close your eyes and be present with your body breathing. You are simply present with what is here in the moment with you. It really just requires a gentle remembering on your part. There's no effort, no practice, no struggle. It's as simple as noticing when you're drifting off into thought, and then very gently bringing yourself back to Presence.

The word *remember* is very significant. I am using the word in a different way than most people are familiar with. Usually, to remember something is to go back into some past event and remember it. But to understand my use of the word, *remember*, we have to go to the word, *dismember*. When we dismember something, we take something that's whole, we cut it and separate it into parts. As we re-member to be present with a flower or a tree or anything else, we are restoring ourselves to Oneness and wholeness. If I am truly present with a flower, I am one part. The flower is the other part. It is in the re-membering, that the parts are restored to wholeness and Oneness is revealed.

Question (male): Thank you, brother Leonard, my name is Kevin. It's been a blessing to be here. Will there be a bridge in the future between Christianity, Islam and Judaism that can bring these three religions to this peaceful Presence?

Leonard's Answer: The only way that these religions can come together in harmony is to open into the present moment. It is in the silence of the present moment that Jew, Christian and Muslim will come out of the illusion that they are separate and open into Oneness. When we come into the silence of the present moment, we come out of the mind. All the spiritual and religious ideas, opinions, traditions, practices and beliefs that separate us simply dissolve as we become fully present and the mind falls silent. As we deepen into Presence, we begin to realize that Judaism, Christianity and Islam are one vine planted by God. The problem is that they've all gone astray. They have disconnected from the truth, and it would be very helpful if they were to reflect upon the role each of these religions was meant to play in the awakening of human consciousness. These three religions are interconnected and interdependent.

Judaism holds the goal of the journey which is deliverance unto the Promised land. But what is the Promised Land? God did not make it clear to Abraham. Jews think it is the land of Israel and Jerusalem. But the Promised Land is not to be found in any one location. It is in all locations. It is Heaven on Earth, and it is only revealed when we reach to a certain level of awakened consciousness. The problem is that the Jews don't know where the goal is and even with the best of intentions, they cannot find it. Now, along comes Jesus who was a Jew. Whether you want to call him the Messiah, a great prophet, a great master or a great teacher, he was a revealer of the Way for the Jews. His life was a demonstration of right relationship with God. His Presence was filled with the Presence of God.

That should have been enough to awaken people at that time, but they were not ready. The words he uttered offer great guidance to those who are ready for the truth. But his words were changed and distorted by those who were trying to establish a following after his death, which has led to a profound misunderstanding of his teaching.

He is not the Savior. He never intended to be the Savior. The need for a Savior is a very real indication of abandonment of responsibility. He was not trying to save anyone. He was trying to wake them up and help them to remember who they are. Each of us is to become our own Savior by becoming present and taking responsibility for whatever arises within us that is not of Presence.

As I said, the Jews have the goal. Jesus was a revealer of the Way. Now let's come to Islam. The essential teaching of Mohammed is that once we have found the Way and reached the goal, how shall we live? Mohammed's answer was very clear and direct. We are to live surrendered to the will of God. Now, I don't imagine that Mohammed meant that we should bow five times each day to some distant city called Mecca. To live a life surrendered to the will of God demands much more than that. The only way to live a surrendered life is to be present, accepting of the present moment as it is and responsive to whatever is occurring in the present moment.

So, what we have finished up with in our world today is rather unfortunate. The Jews have the goal, but they cannot find it. The Christians are followers of the way, but it is not the Way that Jesus was revealing. And Muslims are bowing to God each day, but it is a God of their own creation. If we are to transform our world, we need to transform our religions. It is only when a Jew, a Christian or a Muslim awakens deeply into Presence and silence that they will transcend their religious beliefs and dogma. Only then will they realize the omnipresent nature of God and Oneness. There is only one God. It is the same God, no matter what your religion is.

Male: Thank you.

Leonard: Okay, you're very welcome. Thank you.

Question (female): Is being present a sensual relationship with the present moment?

Leonard's Answer: Yes, of course it's sensual. It's of the senses. You can only be present through your senses. That's the beauty of the human body. It's through your senses that you engage with the present moment, by becoming present with what is here. It is so simple. Be present with what you see, hear, feel, touch, taste or smell. But we humans are so easily distracted. Instead of staying here, fundamentally present with what is here, we go too far into the past and future world of the mind. We have become addicted to thinking. We have become habituated to living in the dream and now nearly the whole of humanity is hopelessly lost there.

Question (female): Thank you. I only heard about this program two hours ago before it started. I came because the description in your promotional material was so in alignment with the path that I'm on. And I'm very glad I did come. I'm in total alignment with what you say. It's like preaching to the converted, but I am wondering if you plan to present this play and this teaching to those who are not in alignment with what you are saying. Would you reach out, for example, to some of the Jewish communities, the Hasidic communities, the Muslim communities?

Leonard: May I respond?

Female: Yes, please.

(*Laughter*)

Leonard's Answer: I would love to take this play and teaching on the road and I would love to address people who are not necessarily open to what I am sharing. But Jesus was aware that his teaching is not for everyone. And so am I. It's only for those who are ready to respond. As Jesus said in the play, "God sent me to find those who are ready to respond."

As I look at you, I have absolutely no doubt that you are deeply responsive to the truth. It will be almost impossible for you not to awaken in this lifetime. You would have to try really hard to go astray.

Female: Thank you.

Leonard's Answer: And one final thing I can say is that I'm not a proselytizer. I'm not seeking to convert anyone or persuade anyone. This is simply an offering and how people respond is not up to me. As long as no one wants to kill me, I am OK with however anyone responds.

(*Laughter*)

Female: Thank you very much.

Leonard: Okay, yes.

Question (male): Leonard, let me congratulate you. What a phenomenally thought-provoking play. I'm so blessed to be here. I've never been more present than right now.

Leonard: Thank you. I am so glad you had this response.

Male: One more comment, if I may. You're play has touched me so deeply, I'm trembling with gratitude. You are such a brave person. Everything you presented in the play just makes so much sense.

Leonard: Beautiful.

Male: Congratulations.

Leonard: Thank you.

Question (female): I would like you to explain a little bit more about the mind, about imagination, intuition and reasoning and how to not get too lost in those areas.

Leonard's Answer: In this teaching I'm not against the mind in any way. I'm not saying the mind should be eliminated, gotten rid of, dissolved, dismissed or dishonored in any way. In fact, the mind is a wonderful instrument of expression. It enables us to express ourselves fully and authentically in the world. I would say that all true creative expression arises from Presence, with the mind acting as an instrument of expression. But it would be very helpful if the mind could be cleared of all those limiting beliefs, judgments and repressed feelings from the past, as well as anxiety about the future. Then the mind would be a pure and unfiltered instrument of expression.

Imagination is a two-edged sword. It can be a vital and necessary element in the creative expression that arises from Presence. But it can also lead us into an imaginary future that we then get lost in. Intuition also has a valuable place in our lives. If we are not fully awakened, then intuition can often arise as insights and realizations that are beyond our conscious awareness. This intuitive knowing is arising from Presence, but as you open more fully into Presence, intuition is replaced by inner knowing.

Reasoning definitely has its place in the world of time. It is a very useful skill to have in navigating the game of life. Of course, we can be over-rational which will lead us further away from the truth and reality of the present moment. However, when it comes to being deeply present, your mind is silent and so there is no reasoning, nor is there anything we need to think about or understand, at least in those moments when we are fully present.

The mind also enables us to play in the world of time. Without the mind, there is no past or future. But with the mind, the remembered past and imagined future exist to give you a sense of who you are and a sense of your life across time.

The problem is that we have all gone too far into the mind. We are so identified with our past memories, future imaginings, ideas, opinions and beliefs that we miss the present moment. We become lost in a kind of dream. When we're in the mind, those limiting beliefs and emotional wounds are a part of our day-to-day life and they radically affect how we think, feel and react to others. They also radically affect and distort our sense of who we are.

In my book *Journey into Now*, I set out very clearly how to heal and release the past and how to open more fully into the present moment. I also share how to integrate awakened consciousness into your day-to-day life and relationships.

Question (female): In the Bible there are scriptures where, after the crucifixion, Jesus came back and actually spoke to his mother and to the disciples. I'd like you to talk a little bit about that and why you didn't include that in the play.

Leonard's Answer: Okay. There are two possibilities in this regard. The story of miracles performed by Jesus could simply have been made up by his disciples to attract followers. But there is also the possibility that he appeared in spiritual form rather than a physical resurrection as Christians believe. To appear in spiritual form is really not that unusual in today's world so it is quite possible that is what happened two thousand years ago. Either way, it doesn't matter in the context of your awakening. Believing that Jesus was resurrected or that he performed miracles will have no influence upon your awakening.

This flower next to me has more power to awaken you than Buddha and Jesus combined. Now why would I say that? Because the flower is here. It is of the present moment and so you can bring yourself present with it. There is no other way to come out of the mind. I am not sure how being present with a memory of Buddha or a belief in Jesus will help you to be more present. It will certainly be comforting, but all belief exists within the mind.

Question (female): I was wondering, why did God make the ego such a challenge?

Leonard's Answer: The ego's resistance to Presence is the main obstacle to the awakening of human consciousness. But what is the ego, what is its role in our lives and how does it function? The ego is not the enemy. To regard the ego as the enemy is one of the greatest mistakes we can make on the spiritual path. We must learn how to come into right relationship with the ego. Only then will we be able to settle into Presence, without being constantly pulled back into the mind by the ego.

If I respond from a more mystical level, I could say that the ego is the first and most devoted servant of God. It is the ego's role to keep us in the separation until it is the right moment to release us back into Presence and Oneness.

The ego needs to be satisfied that you are the true master before it will release you. And who is the true master? It is you, fully present in the moment of now. The true master is that dimension of you that is of this moment and only of this moment. It is the awakened you. It is the I AM presence. It is the I AM that you are.

The ego will not surrender the reins of control until it can depend upon you remaining fundamentally present. And the ego knows that the true master is without judgment, so if it can catch you into the energy of judgment, it will not release you, for it knows that the true master is without judgment.

Question (female): Why is it so difficult for people to reach that level of consciousness you are talking about?

Leonard's Answer: It is very easy to be present. That is not the issue. The issue is that we seem unable to remain present for any length of time and we do not seem to be able to maintain Presence in our day-to-day lives and in our relationships. The reason is clear and simple. We have all become habituated to living in the past and future world of the mind. We are afraid of the unknown and we are comforted by the familiar.

To make it even clearer, we are all addicted to thinking. We cannot stop thinking. One of the first things I will do in one of my retreats is to ask participants to close their eyes, be present with their body breathing and have no thought for sixty seconds. Very few succeed in this endeavor. All thoughts take you into the past or future, and if you believe in those thoughts as being true, you will find yourself imprisoned within the maze that is the world of the mind, with very little access to Presence.

But it does not end there. The ego needs to keep you in the dream, where all the pain from the past is. Its role is to protect you from the pain of living in a world where no one is present. It helps you to repress the painful and difficult emotions, so you won't have to feel them. Then it develops a number of strategies designed to get for you what is missing in your life, like love, acceptance and acknowledgment. The ego will do anything to help you avoid the feeling that you are separate, and it will not surrender its role as your protector easily. You will have to transcend judgment if you are to awaken. So many people seem to be deeply involved in judgment, either as the one judging or the one judged. Judgment will prevent us from settling into Presence.

I've written a book called *Journey into Now,* which is a comprehensive guide to my teaching. In the book, I talk about a two-step dance of awakening. The first step is all about learning the art of being present. The present moment is the doorway to the eternal now. If being present is the first priority in your life, slowly you will deepen into Presence.

The second step involves bringing conscious awareness to all the ways you are involuntarily pulled out of Presence. It involves identifying all the obstacles to your awakening? This second step leads to mastery of the mind and ego. Both Presence and mastery are essential for true awakening.

Male: I wanted to thank you very much. And there are two things I want to share with you. I've often wondered how I can reclaim the innocence, the wonder and the creativity of childhood. And it came to me one day to ask just one question. "Right now, what is obvious?" Somehow that question brought me to this very spacious place of simplicity and beauty. It was like a miracle. I felt the same sense tonight with the calmness of your voice, the way that I was on the very edge of my seat and wondering what you're going to say next. I want to thank you and all I can say is that I feel a profound sense of gratitude for what you do.

Leonard: Well, thank you very much. I really appreciate that.

Question (female): I understand everything you said in the play and I agree with you wholeheartedly, except for the part where you said that Jesus did not perform miracles. I believe that as we awaken into Oneness with God, miracles happen. In my personal life, I have seen a few miracles. One of them happened this evening. I forgot that I had a dead battery and I forgot to charge it before I came over here, and yet it started up immediately. I've seen many miracles like this, and I attribute them to our evolving consciousness and so I believe that Jesus did do all those miracles that they say he did.

Leonard: Okay, may I respond?

Female: Yes.

Leonard's Answer: Thank you for your comment. I totally agree with you that life is full of miracles. A flower blooming is a miracle. A bird soaring through the sky is a miracle. A young child smiling is a miracle. But the greatest miracle of all is to liberate yourself from the dream and awaken into Presence and experience Oneness with God. We have lived and died many times, but not once have we awakened.

Let's assume for a moment that Jesus healed the sick, gave sight to the blind and raised the dead. How many of those that he healed actually awakened? Not one! We get distracted by the stories of healing and miracles. The ego loves those stories, and it would love to have special powers. But it is a distraction from the true teaching of Jesus.

The real purpose of his mission was not to heal the blind or raise the dead, but to wake us up. He was not your Savior. He was a revealer of the Way and what he shared with us two thousand years ago is even more relevant today. Does that ease your concerns?

Female: Yes, I understand you fully now. Thank you. I loved your play.

Leonard: Thank you, and I could see that you were very present throughout the play, which I truly appreciate.

Female: Oh, I loved it.

Leonard: During my performance of the play, it was so wonderful to look out into the audience and see so many who were present. That's why we describe it as not just a play, but as an event in consciousness. If the audience is not present and they're fidgeting or restless, then I'd probably prefer to deliver the whole play to the flowers, because at least they're present.

(Laughter)

The whole point of the play is an invitation into Presence and Oneness. If you experienced it in that way, then the play has been very worthwhile.

Question (male): Yes. Thank you. I'd like you to explain how becoming present contributes towards one's education. We get an education, we become knowledgeable, we develop skills, we plan for our future and we plan our careers. How would all this change as we become more present?

Leonard's Answer: "Seek ye first the kingdom of God, and then all these things shall be added unto you." In other words, if you make being present the first priority in your life, everything else will flow into your life smoothly. There is nothing wrong with education. It is wonderful to be well educated. Study philosophy, psychology, architecture, biology, law or medicine. Or you might choose a life path as a plumber or a carpenter. It doesn't matter. All of it's great. It's all a part of how you can express your authentic self in the world. If you are going to be a doctor, a lawyer, an architect or a psychologist, then be an awakened doctor, lawyer, architect or psychologist. Be an awakened plumber or carpenter. That is what is needed in our world, as long as you're able to disengage from that role you are playing. Then you can instantly return to the silence of the present moment, where you are not playing any role.

To awaken into Presence is not the end of our quest. Most of us have significant blocks to our expression. We must find a level of freedom within ourselves that allows us to express freely and authentically in the world. Ironically, Presence enhances every aspect of expression in your life. Your mind is unburdened as a part of the process of awakening. You will have released that painful, limiting past where you were denied the right to be yourself and express yourself fully and freely. You will have released yourself from judgment, fear and desire. Now you will be motivated by the pursuit of excellence and the ability to express yourself fully, freely and authentically in the world. You will no longer be driven by the need for love, acceptance, approval or recognition. You will no longer be concerned with what others think of you.

You're participating in life from a place of Presence, gratitude and love. When you are present, you are love, strength, clarity, silence, compassion and joy. You're free to be yourself and express yourself freely. Now, if that doesn't enhance the quality of your life, I don't know what will.

Question (female): Do we find Presence through meditation? If not, how do we get to Presence? How do we remain present?

Leonard's Answer: Meditation is great preparation for awakening. The problem with meditation and any kind of spiritual practice can be that, in a very subtle way, you are practicing meditation or some other spiritual practice hoping to get somewhere. Perhaps you just want more peace in your life. Perhaps you are on a path towards enlightenment. Perhaps you are looking for bliss or ecstasy. The problem is that there is a hidden agenda in your practice that is future orientated. You cannot awaken in the future. You cannot be present in the future. You can only be present now, and the great irony is that everything you are hoping to gain by meditation or spiritual practice is already here. You just have to relax into the present moment.

The ego is also involved in preventing you from being present. The ego's world is the past and future. It can never be present. But it will get very involved in your quest for enlightenment, either as the ultimate accomplishment or the ultimate avoidance. Either will succeed in keeping you in the dream.

In order to really awaken, all spiritual practice must be surrendered. All spiritual concepts must be surrendered. All religion must be surrendered. You can go back to those things if you like, but to awaken fully, everything has to be surrendered. For me, everything in physical form is the body of God. If you want to experience the living Presence of God, then bring yourself present with the body of God and you'll start to sense God's Presence in all things present.

Only through the direct experience of God and Presence can the truth be known. It cannot be known from within the mind. You cannot get it from another, whether it's Jesus, Buddha or anyone else. But you can receive guidance. We are all so lost in the maze that is the world of the mind that we most definitely need guidance to free ourselves. There will probably be a need for some healing intervention as it is very difficult to awaken into Presence if you have unresolved emotional wounds and disturbances in your life.

As I referenced in the play, Jesus gave us a clue in this regard.

"Whosoever is angry with his brother, first reconcile with your brother, and then bring the gift to the altar."

He knew that it would be very difficult for his followers to awaken into a deep level of Presence with unresolved issues from the past. But it is worth turning over every stone. Do whatever it takes to awaken yourself from your dream. There is so much here in the present moment waiting to greet you.

The doorway to God is within you. It is at the very heart of silence within you. That's the whole point of the play. Everything you seek is here now and God is within you. That's really the message of Jesus, Buddha, Lao Tzu and Ramana Maharshi. There's no message beyond that. Everything you seek is here now, God is within you and the time of deliverance is now.

Question (male): Leonard, it seems like you had a sudden and spontaneous awakening. I have also heard you speak of a gradual awakening. Can you comment on the difference and which is the most desirable approach?

Leonard's Answer: Occasionally, people will have a sudden awakening like I had, but a sudden awakening can be too much for some people, particularly if they are not well prepared. A sudden awakening can be spontaneous, powerful, multi-dimensional and out of control. With a sudden awakening, there will inevitably be a process of integration, which can at times be quite difficult. And there is always the possibility that the ego will get involved after everything settles down and the ego will be convinced that it is now enlightened. It is very difficult to awaken an enlightened ego.

There are other pitfalls along the way. Many years ago, I was giving an introductory talk in New York City. I was describing how beautiful it can be when we open into the more mystical dimensions of Presence. I was speaking of the Oneness and perfection of the present moment. I was speaking of the intense love that you feel at the deeper levels of Presence. I was speaking about the overwhelming sense of beauty in everything. Just then a man sitting towards the back of the room raised his hand. He was very excited. "I know what you are speaking of," he said. "Thirty years ago, I had an awakening experience exactly like the one you are describing. It was amazing. It was extraordinary. It was the best experience of my life by far."

"That's great," I said.

"And I have been miserable ever since," he added.

"Why have you been so miserable?" I asked, knowing the answer before he responded.

"Because I have been trying to get it back and I can't," he cried.

I then explained that the experience is past. If you try to get it back, that will keep you in the past. And the experience only opened up within you because you had suddenly become present. Don't hold on to anything, including an enlightenment experience. Just be present with whatever is in the moment right now. No past, no future. No holding on. A gradual awakening is much easier. And whether you have a gradual awakening or a sudden awakening, we all finish up in the same place. Here now! A gradual awakening has other advantages. With step one of this teaching, you learn the art of being present. Gradually, it becomes easier and easier to be present and slowly you become established in Presence. But step two of this teaching will guide you into mastery of your own mind and ego. As you bring conscious awareness to your story, who you are in your story, how you get caught in the story and how to release yourself from the story, you are gradually arising in mastery. Who is the true master? It is you in Presence. It is the I AM that you are.

Question (female): I loved your performance in the show. Thank you so much. The ego in our culture right now is often made out to be some kind of villain that we need to get rid of. Is it possible that the ego is performing some role that we are not aware of? Is there another way to view the ego?

Leonard's Answer: As long as we continue to think of the ego in a negative way, we will never awaken. There has to be a dramatic shift in our understanding of the ego. What is the ego? What is its role in our lives? How does it function? How does it keep us in the past and future? Why does it resist any movement into Presence? How do we free ourselves from the ego's resistance? I will briefly answer these questions.

The ego can be described as an independent entity living within your mind, but it does not enter into you from outside. Rather, it is a part of you that originates and develops within you from a fairly early age. It is not to be feared, but rather understood. Its role in your life is to protect you in a painful world where no one is present. It is aware of the limiting beliefs developing within your mind during those early formative years. It is aware of the subtle feeling of being separate that exists within you, mostly at an unconscious level. It is also aware of the difficult feelings you are experiencing, which are too much for a young child to deal with, and so it kicks into action.

Its first job upon your behalf is to help you repress all the painful feelings like anger, hurt, sadness, unfulfilled needs and fear so you won't have to feel them. Then it more or less takes over management of certain aspects of your life. It develops strategies to help you get what it perceives that you need. And it develops strategies to help you avoid a repetition of the pain that you experienced in childhood.

For example, if one of your limiting beliefs is that you are not loved, the ego will do what it can to get you the love that you need. But nothing works! Even if one hundred people are loving you in this moment, you won't let it in because at a deeper level, the unconscious belief that you are not loved prevails until you bring it to consciousness and release it. It is the same if you have a limiting belief that you are not accepted, or that you are not good enough. Nothing works and eventually the ego becomes frustrated and begins harassing you to improve yourself so that you will be loved, accepted and considered good enough. In a very strange way, the ego thinks it is motivating you to improve yourself by being hard on you and criticizing and judging you. But it is a very ineffective motivational strategy. It just does not work. Beating or verbally abusing a child will bring out the worst in a child rather than the best.

How does the ego function? How does it keep you out of Presence? It is very simple. The only way that the ego can have any control or influence over you is to generate thoughts and feelings that are designed to catch you into the past or future. All it has to do is bring up a thought involving resentment. That thought will come with an associated feeling. If you believe in that thought as being true, you will be immediately caught in the past. Thoughts that have a theme of revenge, blame, guilt, regret or anger will also keep you in the past. If you believe in these thoughts and act upon them in any way, you will be caught in the past.

On the other hand, you can simply witness the thought. Do not be for or against the thought. Don't believe in the thought and just as importantly, do not judge or reject the thought. Remain indifferent to the thought. It has no meaning unless you give it meaning by believing in it or rejecting it. If you are simply an impartial witness to the thought as it arises, then you will remain present and the thought will simply dissolve.

The ego has a brilliant trick to keep you imprisoned in an imaginary and illusory future. It is such a clever trick and we all fall for it, year after year, lifetime after lifetime. It is the promise of future fulfillment. When you get a new dress, a new car or a new husband, you will be happy. When you become enlightened you will be fulfilled. These are false promises that are designed to keep you in the world of the mind.

However, in order to witness the thoughts and feelings as they arise, you will have to first open into Presence. There is no other way! When you are present, you have transcended the mind and the ego. It is from this transcendent perspective of Presence that you can easily witness the thoughts and feelings as they arise, and you can gently disengage from them and remain present.

Another key to liberation is to come into right relationship with the ego, which is only possible from Presence. When you are present, you are love, acceptance and compassion. This is the energy that you can bring to the ego. The ego thrives on judgment, rejection and struggle. It is not familiar with being loved, appreciated and accepted. It doesn't know what to do with that. If you can remain fairly consistently present and relate to the ego with love, acceptance and compassion, sooner or later the ego will begin to relax and ultimately surrender. But it is surrender with honor. For this to occur, you will have to be present and come into right relationship with the ego.

When Jesus journeyed into the desert for forty days and forty nights, he suddenly projected his ego outside of him, although he was not aware that it was his ego that he was encountering. It appeared to him like a little devil trying to tempt him. But because the ego was projected outside of him, he was able to see and hear what it was up to, and so he could say no. Had his ego not projected outside of him, he might have fallen victim to its temptation.

So, two thousand years later, we have a choice. We can fast for forty days and forty nights and hope that we will have the same hallucination as Jesus. Or we can simply become present and it is from Presence that we can be a witness to thoughts as they arise. We can be a witness to the subtle movements and temptations of the ego designed to keep you out of Presence. Slowly the ego's role in your life will be transformed. When it recognizes the true master arising from within, it will surrender and it will no longer seek to pull you out of Presence.

Question (male): What level of Presence is necessary to open into Oneness with God?

Leonard's Answer: There is a level of Presence where you begin to sense the Presence of God in all things present. It's a perfect vibration of consciousness that reveals Oneness. This is where we experience the expression, "I am that I am."

There are different ways of relating to those words. If your eyes are closed and you are in a state of perfect Presence, which can best be described as pure consciousness, then you may declare, "I am that silent Presence of Pure Consciousness. I am that. I am." Of course, those words are spoken from Presence and silence.

When you are so deeply present with a flower or a tree that you feel one with the flower or tree, then you can declare, "I am that flower, or I am that tree. I am that. I am." It is as if you are a mirror for existence. At this deep level of Presence, you are consciousness reflecting consciousness to itself. You are Is-ness reflecting Is-ness to itself.

It is very difficult to find God as Creator, but it is very easy to find God as Creation. Everything in physical form is the body of God. Bring yourself present with the body of God and you will begin to experience God as the silent Presence in all things present. If you feel Oneness with a tree, then whether you know it or not, you are in a state of Oneness with God. It is that simple.

Question (male): Earlier tonight, you were talking about beliefs. You said we have to get beyond our fundamental beliefs if we are to know the truth. How do we do that?

Leonard's Answer: There are two dimensions of you. There is that dimension of you which is fully awake in the moment of Now. This is the truth of who you are. It is the awakened you, transcendent of the mind and transcendent of time. You are aware of the Oneness of all things. You feel peaceful, silent, loving and grateful.

And then there is that dimension of you living in the mind and the world of time. The problem is that your mind has been programmed with limiting beliefs, most of which originate in your early childhood. And these limiting beliefs affect every aspect of your life and relationships. The world of time is nothing more than your remembered past and imagined future, which give you a sense of who you are, but it is not the truth of who you are. You have to awaken into Presence to know the truth of who you are.

The present moment is transcendent of the mind, and so it is from Presence that you can gradually identify all your limiting beliefs and repressed feelings. All you have to do is be sufficiently present, pay attention and notice the thoughts or feelings arising within you.

Now, I'll give you a clue. We all share the same limiting beliefs. You can take your pick, there's so many of them. I am all alone, there is no one here for me, I'm abandoned, I'm separate, I am not seen, I'm not good enough, I'm not wanted, I'm not loved, I'm not worthy, I don't count, there must be something wrong with me, life is a struggle, I can't have what I want, I have to please others, I'm not accepted as I am, I'm not free to be myself, I can't express myself freely, I can't do it, I can't express my feelings and I don't want to be here.

If your parents weren't present with you and were not unconditionally loving, then more than likely you have at least three or four of these limiting beliefs programmed into you mind, and probably a lot more. And to varying degrees, you are most likely living with repressed feelings like anger, hurt, sadness, unfulfilled needs and fear.

These limiting beliefs and repressed emotions can only affect you when they remain buried in the darkness of your unconscious mind. As you bring these things to conscious awareness, they gradually lose their power over you. Sometimes a healing of some traumatic experience from the past is necessary to release you more fully into the present moment. The important thing is to not be for or against the limiting beliefs, repressed feelings or whatever else arises from within the dream. Just be present and pay attention.

Whatever arises is simply to be revealed within awakened consciousness, and it is to be revealed with love, acceptance, compassion and a complete absence of judgment. I suggest that the best approach is to simply own, acknowledge and confess whatever is arising. Just bring it to conscious awareness. Own! Acknowledge! Confess! Don't judge!

Question (male): In one of your online videos, I've heard you speak about substitute needs. Could you explain what you mean by that?

Leonard's Answer: When you were in your mother's womb and immediately after you were born, you were a very present little Being. You were innocent in the true sense of the word. Your mind was not filled with thoughts, ideas, concepts and beliefs.

When Jesus said that only those who are like children can enter the Kingdom, he was not telling us to be childish. He was referring to the mind of a very young child, which had not yet been programmed and filled with other people's ideas and beliefs. He is really speaking of a silent mind, free of thought, opinion and belief.

When you were in your mother's womb, you were connected to her in every way. We could say that it was an experience of Oneness in the womb. But then you were born. You went through the most traumatic experience of separation that you will ever have to endure. In order for you to recover from that experience of separation called birth, you needed your parents and those around you to be very present, because you were already deeply present as you emerged from the womb. Had they been fully present with you, attending to your every need in Presence, you would have recovered from the trauma of the birth experience. The feeling of being separate would not have developed within you.

But your parents were not present. It was not their fault. No one had shown them how to be present. By the time you were born, your parents were well and truly absorbed into the world of the mind. They were not present and so the trauma of separation that you experienced in the birth process never really healed. It is still there within each one of us, and we experience it as a subtle feeling of emptiness within the body. This feeling of being separate is painful. We don't want to feel the emptiness and so we develop all sorts of strategies to help us to escape the feeling that we are separate.
But in so doing, we take ourselves further into separation, as we become absorbed into the past and future world of the mind. And we take ourselves further away from the experience of Oneness, which is the only thing that will truly heal us and release us from the illusion that we are separate.

It is for this reason that I say that the true and original need is Presence. We need others to be present with us. If someone is present with you, then you can feel the energy of love, acceptance and Oneness emanating from that other. And this is all you really need.

However, very few are present in our world. It is painful and so, at an early age, we embark on a journey that will take us further and further into the illusion of separation. It is a journey in pursuit of the substitute needs. The first substitute need is love. If your parents are not present, then in order to feel safe, you need to feel loved. But it is really the unconditional love that arises from Presence that you need. Instead, you received conditional love which was not enough to release you from the feeling that you are separate and so you began to look for love from others. It is possible to spend the rest of your life looking for love, but it is a fruitless endeavor. Even if one hundred people love you in this moment, you will not let it in. You will not feel it because at a deeper level, your mind is programmed with the limiting belief that you are not loved.

Whenever you look to others for love, it means that you are caught in a dream and in the dream, you are not loved. It also means that you are not present, for if you were present you would know that you are love. Why would you need love if you are love? To pursue love within the dream takes you further into the dream. It takes you further into the illusion that you are separate.

It is really the same with acceptance, which is the second substitute need. If no one is present with you, and you do not feel the unconditional love coming from your parents, then at least you will need to feel accepted in order to feel safe. But it is the unconditional acceptance that arises from Presence that you need.

Conditional acceptance will not heal you. Seeking acceptance from others simply means that you are caught in the dream and in the dream, you are not accepted. You are not worthy and you are not good enough. These are just more of the limiting beliefs that developed during childhood. In Presence, there is no judgment. In Presence, you are the energy of acceptance and the need to be accepted simply fades away.

The third and final substitute need is the need to be special, which includes the need to be recognized and acknowledged. If I am richer than you, more successful than you, more beautiful than you, then you will notice me. You will think I am worthwhile. In Presence, there is no need to be special. In Presence, everyone is equal, everyone is special.

The real solution is to not try to fix the dream, but rather to awaken out of the dream. This means that you will have to bring the dream into the full light of consciousness as you become more and more present. You will have to bring the limiting beliefs and repressed feelings to consciousness, for it is these limiting beliefs and repressed feelings that drive you to pursue the substitute needs.

If you want to awaken, you will have to bring to consciousness all the ways that you lose yourself in the pursuit of these substitute needs, looking for love, acceptance and approval. You will have to return to the true and original need, which can be summed up in the following way, "You don't have to love me. You don't have to accept me or think I am special. But I do need you to be present with me. If you are here, I can be here, which is all I really want or need."

For those who are ready for the last step, then say this, "I would like you to be here with me, but actually I am here whether you are here or not!"

Question (male): What happens when you know you are in the mind? You want to be present but your mind refuses to calm down.

Leonard's Answer: Many of us are caught in constant, unintended and unconscious thinking. All thoughts take you into the past or future and so if the thoughts never stop, you will find yourself continually absorbed into the past and future world of the mind. And if you believe in your thoughts as somehow being true, then you will find yourself imprisoned within the mind.

This is what has happened to humanity. It is largely because we are reluctant to feel any kind of pain. In early childhood, we decided that the feelings were too painful and too difficult to allow ourselves to feel. This includes feelings like anger, hurt, sadness, unfulfilled need and fear and so we repressed the feelings. We used the ability to think as our avenue of escape from these painful feelings, including the feelings of isolation and separation.

By thinking, we can take ourselves out of whatever is happening into an imaginary and illusory world based in the past or future. Gradually this became a habit and we slowly became habituated to functioning within the world of the mind. This occurred to each one of us during our early formative years in this lifetime, but it happened at a collective level for humanity over many lifetimes.

We do not realize that we are living in a kind of dream made up of our past memories and future imaginings, together with all our opinions, ideas, concepts and beliefs. And to make the situation worse, we have all become addicted to thinking. It is the greatest addiction and we can't stop thinking, which means that we are always in the mind, disconnected from the present moment.

We have to recognize that the pain that we are trying to escape from is from the past and is not happening now. If we want to free ourselves from the dream and open into Presence, we will have to feel and express our feelings in a conscious and responsible way.

We will have to come into right relationship, not only with our feelings, but also with the ego, the inner child and every aspect of who we have become living in the world of the mind. And we will have to become sufficiently present so that we can be aware of our thoughts as they arise, without rejecting the thoughts or believing in them. In this way, we will gradually arise in mastery of the mind and ego.

The mind will calm down as you become present. The thoughts will slow down and eventually come to a stop. You will open into an entirely new dimension of yourself. You will open into peace, silence, love and Oneness. You will no longer be concerned with what others think of you. You will no longer judge yourself or others. You will feel free to be yourself and express yourself fully and freely as the unique Being that you are.

Question (male): How can we defeat the ego?

Leonard's Answer: You cannot defeat the ego. The ego thrives on judgment, rejection, and struggle. The only thing that will bring the ego to a place of relaxation and surrender is the energy of love and acceptance and that is not difficult when you are present. When you are present, you are the energy of love and acceptance, so first you will have to become present. Then you will have to bring conscious awareness to how your ego functions, how it manipulates you and tries to deceive you. The ego has a bag of tricks to keep you in its world of the past and future where it is in control.

It keeps you in the past by bringing up thoughts involving anger, blame, guilt, regret and resentment, which usually come with an associated feeling. If you believe in any of these thoughts or feelings, or reject any of these thoughts or feelings, it's got you. Now you are in the past and the ego is in control. And it can easily tempt you into the future with the promise of future fulfillment.

The ego does not care whether you are in the past or future, as long as you are not present, for when you are present the ego is no longer in control.

From Presence, we gently and lovingly witness the thoughts and feelings generated by the ego. We have compassion and even gratitude for the ego. It has been protecting us all these years against the pain of living in a world where no one is present.

We do not judge the ego in any way and we have no thought or intention to get rid of the ego. We simply become more aware of its subtle manipulations. And I'll tell you a little secret. The ego is actually waiting for the arrival of the true master arising from within. The true master is that dimension of you that is fully awake in the moment of Now. It is the I AM of you, that eternal silent Presence of Pure Consciousness at the very center of your Being.

The ego will test you before it will release you more fully into Presence. The test is a very simple and precise test and it's a test that almost everyone on the planet fails over and over again. The test is the test of judgment. The ego will bring up thoughts and feelings involving judgment. The ego knows that the true master is without judgment, so if it can catch you into the energy of judgment then it knows that you are not the true master and that it is not the right time to release you. It is impossible to pass the ego's test unless you are fully present because it is only in Presence that you are without judgment. The moment you re-enter the dream, you will notice just how much judgment is a part of your life in the world of time.

Question (male): How do we pass the ego's test?

Leonard's Answer: It is actually very simple. If you notice the energy of judgment arising, do not judge it. Do not try and stop it. Just acknowledge that judgment is arising. Be neutral. Be playful. Just say "judging" in a very light and playful way. You are letting the energy of judgment know that you are aware of it, but you are not judging it or even trying to get rid of it. If you do find yourself caught in the energy of judgment and you cannot disengage from it, then play with it. Ham it up. Be judgmental. Be very judgmental. Ride that judgment horse until the horse is satisfied and then let it go. Come back to Presence and peace.

Question (female): I wanted to ask about collective suffering, like humanity's suffering. Should we do something to alleviate the suffering of the masses?

Leonard's Answer: Of course, we should respond spontaneously and authentically with compassion, generosity and kindness. But the response should be coming from Presence. If you respond from a place of fear or anger, then you become a part of the problem.

There are two important things to be aware of when responding to human suffering. The first is the clear realization that all human suffering is a result of human unconsciousness. It's because we're all lost in the mind and disconnected from Presence that we suffer. When we're lost in the mind, we are governed by our own egos.

The ego's basic position is:

- Me, me, me!
- Mine, mine, mine!
- I'm right, I'm right I'm right!
- What's in it for me?
- What do I get out of this?
- How can I use this for myself?
- How can I take advantage of this?

Now there are more than seven billion egos on this planet living under the control and influence of the ego. What will the outcome be if we continue to live this way? The greatest service you can contribute to end the suffering of humanity is your own awakening. That's the real solution. And if enough of us awaken, it will create a ripple effect at the collective level, which will eventually lead to the collective awakening of humanity.

The whole point of the human journey is not to fix or improve the dream, but to awaken out of the dream. We can end all suffering in our lives simply by recognizing a simple and fundamental truth.

"In truth, there is no life outside of this moment."

If you recognize this simple truth and you recognize that you have been lost in a dream for most of your life, then you greatly increase your chance of awakening from that dream. The dream does not have to go away. We just have to stop believing in it as somehow being true. And we have to abide in the truth that is always available to us when we are present. Now let's all relax and have a moment together in Presence.

Question (male): How do we stop that mind chatter, which just keeps going and going and going?

Leonard's Answer: First of all, it is important to recognize that we humans have become habituated to living in the dream. We have been relating to the world and each other from within the mind, lifetime after lifetime. It is what we are used to. To leave the past and future and become present is to enter the unknown. Most people are afraid of the unknown and prefer to remain in the dream, no matter how miserable it is. Therefore, we have to ask ourselves, "What level of intention and what level of commitment will it take to free ourselves from these habitual patterns and become present?"

To make matters worse, we are all addicted to thinking. It is the greatest addiction. The thoughts just keep arising even when we are not intending to think. If there is a constant stream of unconscious and unintended thought, then you will always be in the past and future world of the mind.

There is only one way to overcome this addiction. First learn the art of being present. Presence is transcendent of the past and future. It is transcendent of the mind. This enables you to be a witness to whatever is arising within the mind from a transcendent perspective. You can be a witness to the thoughts as they arise. The most important thing is to not judge the thoughts or try to stop them. Simply notice the thought arising and gently return to Presence without any judgment or rejection of the thought. You are neutral towards the thought. You do not believe in the thought, but nor do you reject it. However, it can be very difficult for some people to overcome this addiction to thinking.

Has anybody been practicing meditation for thirty years and yet the mind keeps on chattering? There is a very subtle reason for this! When we're practicing meditation or engaged in any other kind of spiritual practice, there is a very subtle future agenda involved.

You cannot awaken in the future. You can only awaken now. Why is that? Because there is no future. Past and future belong to the dream. There is only now. The present moment is already here. Seeking the present moment will keep you in the future. So just relax and be present with what is already here in the present moment with you. I'm not saying that practicing meditation is not beneficial. It can be immensely beneficial. I am simply saying that in order to become established in Presence, then you have to go beyond the notion of a future outcome and accept the present moment as it is.

Question (male): Jesus had disciples. What is the value of being a disciple in today's world?

Leonard's Answer: What I say is become a disciple unto the present moment. Let the present moment be your master. And for me, the present moment and God are one and the same, so become a disciple to God. This means that you are disciplined in returning to Presence whenever you notice that you have drifted into the past and future world of thought and disconnected from the present moment. What I usually suggest is that whenever it is appropriate for you to think, then think. When there is no need to be thinking, then be present. There's no need to think when you're washing the dishes. There is no need to think when you are putting the garbage out. There is no need to think if you are going for a walk. You would be much better off being present as you wash the dishes or go for a walk.

Now let me say one final thing in response to you. There is absolutely nothing wrong with thinking. There's nothing wrong with the world of the mind. There's nothing wrong with having memories and planning into the future. You could not function in the world of time without thinking. Just do not get lost in a world of endless thought. Do not believe in your thoughts, beliefs, opinions and ideas as truth. Only when you are present do you enter the truth. Make the present moment the foundation of your life. Presence is a solid and very strong foundation for your life within the world of time.

Question (male): Can you talk about the ego a little bit more? Ego seems to have developed its own persona and there's a widely held belief that if we had the ability to kill the ego then we'd be more connected to God.

Leonard's Answer: If you intend to kill the ego or get rid of the ego in any way, you will remain eternally enslaved by the ego. You cannot defeat the ego for the simple reason that the one trying to defeat the ego is the ego itself. It is one of the ego's tricks to keep you under its control. To try to get rid of the ego is a judgment of the ego, and all judgment takes you out of Presence.

So, how do we free ourselves from the control and domination of our own egos. There is only one way. We must come into right relationship with the ego and that is only possible when you are present. When you are present, you are the energy of love, acceptance and compassion and it is this energy of love, acceptance and compassion that you bring to the ego. You now know that the ego is not the enemy. In fact, it is your friend and protector. It has been protecting you all these years against the pain of living in a world where no one is present. If you have a limiting belief that you are not loved or you are not accepted, it is trying different strategies to get you the love and acceptance that it thinks you need. If you have a limiting belief that you are not good enough, the ego will develop strategies to prove to others that you are good enough.

The problem is that none of the ego's strategies work. Even if many people are loving you in this moment, you will not feel it. You will not let it in because at a deeper and more unconscious level, you have the limiting belief that you are not loved. That limiting belief will prevail until you bring it to consciousness and stop believing in it. Eventually, the ego becomes frustrated with you. It judges and criticizes you as a way of motivating you to be better. But that approach does not work either.

If you try to fix yourself from within the dream, you are affirming that the dream is real, and you will become even more absorbed into the dream. But if you simply recognize the dream for what it is, then slowly you will begin to relax out of the dream as you open into Presence.

Question (male): First, thank you so much Leonard. I just absolutely love your play and I'm so glad you made a video recording of this because I would like to see it a number of times to really absorb all of the fine details. I do have a question. Did Jesus perform miracles, like changing water into wine?

Leonard's Answer: Did he walk across the water? Absolutely not. Did he change water into wine? Certainly not. Ridiculous! Did he change stones into loaves of bread? Absurd. It's ridiculous. You see, those stories were invented to attract followers after his death on the cross. Most likely, no one would have been attracted to his teaching after his death, without miracles and myths to believe in. The greatest miracle is to awaken from the dream and be fully present.

Question (male): Do you believe that we need some sort of a universal moral code so that we treat each other with kindness and respect.

Leonard's Answer: When you become truly present, there is no need for a moral code. It's absolutely unnecessary. When you're deeply present and experiencing Oneness, then you open up to those words of Jesus when he said, "Love thy neighbor as thyself."

Now perhaps he should have expanded those words to include, "Love thy neighbor as thyself, because thy neighbor IS thyself." And your neighbor is not limited to your human neighbor. It extends to every mountain, every tree, every flower, every bird, every animal and creature of the sea. When you're truly present, you would not chop down one tree, let alone a whole forest, without deep contemplation. And you would make sure that whatever replaces that tree enhances the natural beauty of God's world.

If you are aware of the Oneness of all things, there is no need for morality. The Ten Commandments are rendered irrelevant. In Presence, you would act in a way that honors and reflects the words of Jesus, when he said, "Do unto others as you would have them do unto you."

Question (male): How do we awaken into Oneness?

Leonard's Answer: It is very simple. You open into Oneness by becoming present. As you become more deeply present, your mind will calm down. Thoughts will slow down and eventually stop. If you remain present, without expectation and with a loving, generous and grateful heart, Oneness will be revealed. But a pre-requisite is that you surrender believing in your thoughts, opinions and beliefs as somehow being true.

Male: It's difficult to surrender belief in your thoughts.

Leonard: That is just a thought and it is not true. If you believe in that thought, then it will be difficult. Confess that thought and then let it go. That thought is based in the past. It is probably based in one or more of the limiting beliefs, like "life is a struggle, I can't do it and I am a failure." Those limiting beliefs will affect every aspect of your life including the degree to which you will awaken in this lifetime.

Question (male): Hello Leonard. My name is Rick. I'd like to thank you for your great contribution to the awakening of consciousness and I hope that your message continues to get out to multitudes of people. Now I have a question for you. It seems likely that the great founders of all the religions of the world experienced this Presence that you are speaking of today. Does that seem likely to you?

Leonard's Answer: It seems absolutely likely to me. How could it be otherwise? Whether it's Buddha, Lao Tzu, Jesus or Ramana, the truth emerges from the silence within them. That same truth is available for everyone right now. But it exists at the very heart of silence within you. It exists at the center of your Being. That is where God is. That is where the eternal is.

Now, if you are lost in the mind, living in separation and illusion, you are denied access to that level of truth. Instead of awakening into the truth, we keep building up more knowledge, philosophies and religions within the mind as a substitute for the truth. The truth is already here. It is always here. Awakening simply reveals the truth in all its fullness. It reveals Oneness. Right now, as I look at you from Presence, I'm seeing so many dimensions of you. It's impossible to describe. You're an awakened being in this moment and you're not doing anything. You're just here. We are all amazing Beings on an amazing journey. So it's really time for those who are ready to awaken.

As each one of us awakens, it's like dropping a stone into a dark pond of human unconsciousness - ripples of light! If enough of us awaken, it will impact the collective.

Awakening is quite ordinary. It is your natural state. It simply means you're in the truth of life rather than lost in a world of illusion. You're fundamentally present rather than fundamentally absent. Sometimes the present moment is extraordinary and you open into the most extraordinary experience of Oneness, love and perfection.

Question (female): During the play, you referred to Buddha. Could you comment on the similarities and differences between Buddha and Jesus?

Leonard's Answer: Jesus was a living demonstration of who we are when we're awake in Oneness with God. Buddha was a living example of one who has awakened to the very peak of human consciousness. Both Buddha and Jesus were reflections of who we really are.

Our destiny is not to be Christians or Buddhists. Our destiny is far greater than that.

> Don't be a Buddhist. Be a Buddha.
> Don't be a Christian. Be a Christ.

If Buddha and Jesus were sitting next to me right now, they would be nodding vigorously in agreement.

"Yes of course," they would say. "What else do you think we were saying?"

Buddha is not a person. Buddha is a state of awakened consciousness. After many years of seeking, Gautama the man awakened to Buddha consciousness and in that moment he became the Buddha. It is the same with Jesus. Christ is not a person. Christ is a state of consciousness. Jesus the man awakened into Christ consciousness and in that moment he became the Christ. If you awaken to the same level of Presence as Buddha, then you would be awake in Buddha consciousness. If you awaken to the same level of Presence as Jesus, then you would be a Christ.

It is important to know that both Buddha and Christ consciousness exist fully and completely within you right now. It is not something that you accomplish or achieve. Just relax, deepen into Presence and you will discover Buddha and Christ within you. Buddha and Christ consciousness are remarkably similar. Buddha consciousness is essentially a state of pure consciousness. At the deepest level, it is a state of pure consciousness beyond form and content. Buddha referred to it as 'Samadhi.' Buddha emerged out of India, and because there were so many deities in Indian spirituality, Buddha chose to not emphasize God in his teaching. Jesus emerged out of a very different culture. He was a Jew. In Judaism, there is only one God and Jesus saw himself as one with God, but also in service to God. His relationship with God was both personal and impersonal.

Both Buddha and Jesus were immersed in eternal Oneness and Is-ness. There's only one Is-ness. It's the same Is-ness in the flowers, in the trees, in the space all around us. It is the same Is-ness that Jesus and Buddha awakened into. We exist within this Is-ness and this Is-ness exists within us. There's only one Is-ness and you're in it right now. This is it.

Question (male): Thanks, Leonard. In the present moment, the world is a wonderful, miraculous, interconnected place, but it's also inhabited by billions of egos that seem to be destroying the earth. Is it possible for us, on a global scale, to awaken in consciousness and change the course that our unconsciousness has set us on?

Leonard's Answer: It is absolutely possible. Indeed, it is everyone's destiny to awaken fully. Not only that, our destiny is actually pre-determined the moment we are conceived in our mother's womb. It is not unlike an acorn. The acorn's destiny is also pre-determined. Its destiny is inevitable. It has no option other than to evolve into an oak tree.

It's the same with us. Our ultimate destiny is inevitable. Sooner or later we will evolve into Buddha and Christ consciousness. It is as inevitable as the acorn evolving into the oak tree. There's no way around it. However, there is a significant difference between us and the acorn. We have been given free will and that enables us to take as many side tracks as we choose. This can dramatically delay the unfolding of our destiny. We've taken so many side tracks into the world of the mind that now we are lost there and we can't find our way back to Oneness and God. It reminds me of the story of the prodigal son that Jesus spoke of and the joy that arises whenever the prodigal son (or daughter) find their way back to God.

Now, how can we find our way back to God? It is very simple. Just learn the art of being present and arise in mastery of the mind and ego. The present moment is the doorway to God and Oneness. If you stand at the doorway long enough, God will come to greet you. Once humanity has awakened in consciousness, there will be no more cruelty, abuse, inequality or injustice in our world. There will be peace, love, harmony and a sense of the Oneness of all things.

Question (male): What is the soul and how does it fit into everything you are sharing with us?

Leonard's Answer: You are a multi-dimensional Being. You exist at various dimensions of consciousness simultaneously. One of those dimensions is the soul dimension. The soul is that dimension of you that has been on a journey over many lifetimes.

Before the journey began, you existed in the heavenly realm. It was all you ever knew. There was no separation and you existed in perfect Oneness with God and all that is. In the heavenly realm, there is no physical form. It is a formless existence but you could manifest whatever you wanted in Heaven. You created your own reality and experience of Heaven, but it was always in Oneness and perfect harmony with God. Although you could manifest the appearance of form, it was always a formless existence.

Then the soul's journey began. There was a shift from Oneness into duality. There was a shift from the eternal Now into the past and future. There was a shift from a formless world to the world of form. There was a shift from the experience of Oneness into the experience of separation. We did not like this shift into separation. It felt like we had been ejected from Heaven and so we judged it. The moment we entered into judgment, we locked ourselves into separation and closed the door to Oneness.

We have lived many lifetimes since that original fall in consciousness, continually trying to find our way back to God and Oneness. However, with each lifetime, we became more lost in separation. We got more and more absorbed into the world of the mind. We got more involved in judgment. We became addicted to thinking. We held onto our beliefs more rigidly. We got caught up in fear, false power and greed. And we disconnected from our true nature. The soul believes that it must purify itself if it is to find its way back to God and be restored to Oneness.

The soul believes that it must learn certain lessons and find answers to certain questions, which will propel the soul towards its ultimate destination of a return to Oneness. That's where you come in. You are that part of your soul that has incarnated into physical form is this lifetime. The soul is like a river flowing over many lifetimes. You are like a stream that broke off from the river to journey through one lifetime. The stream is in service to the river.

You are here upon behalf of the soul to discover who you really are and you are here to find answers to certain questions:

* What is the true nature of love?
* What is the true nature of acceptance?
* What is the true nature of power?
* What is the true nature of compassion?
* In truth, who are you and what is your life's purpose?

In this way, you are the champion of your soul and the soul will be profoundly affected by your experiences in this lifetime. Did you learn your lessons upon behalf of the soul? Have your efforts in this lifetime advanced the soul towards its own immortality? Or have you failed to learn your lessons and have you therefore taken the soul into even more separation?

The truth is that almost everyone on the planet has failed in this endeavor. We are just as lost as we have always been. Even the soul made a very significant mistake. The soul is unaware that there is a master lesson that instantly reveals answers to all the other questions. The master lesson is this. The present moment is the doorway to God and the Eternal. The present moment reveals Oneness and Heaven on Earth. That which you seek is here now. You cannot awaken in the future. You can only awaken now. The soul is unaware of the master lesson, and so you are the one who must find your way to the master lesson. Each moment you are truly present, the soul comes into alignment with you in Presence.

But when you get caught back into the dream, the soul is caught back into its dream. This continues over and over again, until you finally free yourself from the dream and settle into Presence and Oneness. Eventually, you will be so grounded in the present moment that it will feel like you have come home. The soul will rejoice, because as you find you way home to Presence, Oneness, God and Heaven on Earth, the soul finds its way home.

Question (female): How does being present benefit us in our day-to-day life?

Leonard's Answer: As you become more and more present, you will find yourself liberated from the dream. The dream is still there but you are no longer identified with it. You know that it is all an illusion and the feeling of being separate dissolves as you gradually open into Oneness. The limiting beliefs lose their power over you. You have been through a process of liberating the repressed emotions, which will bring a much greater level of peace and freedom into your life. You no longer judge yourself or others. You are no longer concerned by what others think of you. You feel free to be yourself and express yourself freely. Of course you can still think, but now your thinking is much clearer, because you are not burdened by pain from the past or anxiety about the future.

When you are present, you are quite literally the energy of love. It has nothing to do with who or what you love. You are love and you emanate love in the same way that a candle emanates light. You are also the energy of acceptance and compassion and you are empowered from within. Can you imagine how your life will change as all these qualities of Presence begin to flow into your life?

When I first started this teaching, it was very difficult to bring people into Presence. Many years later, it is so much easier. I have also observed that more and more people are having awakening experiences and many more are interested in awakening and Presence. This is great news, because it is absolutely necessary that humanity as a species awakens.

True awakening involves not only becoming fundamentally established in Presence, but also arising in mastery of your mind and ego. I hope and pray that my answers to your questions will support, encourage and guide you on your path of awakening.

ABOUT THE AUTHOR

Leonard Jacobson is a modern mystic and awakened spiritual teacher who is deeply committed to guiding and supporting others in their journey towards wholeness.

He was born in Melbourne, Australia and was educated at the University of Melbourne, graduating with a law degree in 1969. In 1981, he experienced the first of a series of spontaneous mystical awakenings that profoundly altered his perception of life, truth, and reality. Each of these enlightenment experiences revealed deeper and deeper levels of consciousness, filling his teachings and his writings with wisdom, clarity, love and compassion.

He has been running workshops and seminars for almost four decades, offering inspiration and guidance to those on a path of awakening. He offers regular teaching sessions, weekend workshops, and longer residential retreats in the United States, Europe, Japan, China and Australia.

He is the founder of The Conscious Living Foundation, a registered non-profit organization. In 2005, he was awarded the Peace Prize by Religious Science International, although he is not affiliated or associated with any religion. His teaching is both inclusive of and transcendent of all religions and spiritual traditions. It is for all those genuinely seeking to awaken, and for all those who do not yet realize that they are genuinely seeking to awaken.

For more information on upcoming events, to access free teaching materials or to sign up for our mailing list, please visit www.leonardjacobson.com

OTHER BOOKS BY LEONARD JACOBSON

Words from Silence
An Invitation to Spiritual Awakening
Revised edition
ISBN No 978-1-890580-06-3

This powerful book reveals many of the hidden keys to awakening, offering clear guidance to those on a spiritual path. Each page is a lyrically beautiful expression of an essential truth. Zen-like in its simplicity, it communicates directly with the heart and soul of the reader, gently inviting a response from the deepest level of Presence.

To order a copy of Words from Silence,
Visit www.leonardjacobson.com

OTHER BOOKS BY LEONARD JACOBSON

Embracing the Present
Living an Awakened Life
Revised edition
ISBN No 978-1-890580-10-0

Embracing the Present casts a bright light upon the path of awakening. With great clarity, the author leads us through the maze of the mind and its illusory world of the past and future into the real and illumined world of the present moment. He shares with us how to be fully present and how to integrate awakened consciousness into our everyday lives and our relationships.

The present moment, he tells us, is the doorway to God. It is the true source of love, truth, power and freedom. He writes in a profoundly simple and poetic style that speaks directly to the heart and soul of the reader. To read this powerful and challenging book is to embark upon a mystical journey, which will touch you deeply and bring fullness and completion into your life. To awaken into the present moment is like coming home. It is like waking up out of a long dark dream and finding yourself in Heaven on Earth.

To order a copy of Embracing the Present,
Visit www.leonardjacobson.com

OTHER BOOKS BY LEONARD JACOBSON

Bridging Heaven & Earth
A Return to Oneness
Revised edition
ISBN No 978-1-890580-09-4

Bridging Heaven & Earth is intended to awaken you. To read this book is to embark upon a journey of awakening, which will touch you deeply and bring fullness and completion into your life. The author takes us on a mystical tour of human consciousness, covering such diverse topics as liberation from the mind and ego, awakening into Presence, the soul's journey, the soul's lessons, keys to spiritual awakening, the universal laws of life, the essential nature of Being, Christ consciousness, God consciousness, the eternal dilemma of God, and so much more.

To order a copy of Bridging Heaven & Earth,
Visit www.leonardjacobson.com

OTHER BOOKS BY LEONARD JACOBSON

Journey into Now
Clear Guidance on the Path of Spiritual Awakening
ISBN: Hard cover: 978-1-890580-03-2
Paperback: 978-1-890580-04-9

With perfect precision, the author guides the reader along a path of awakening that leads to liberation from the pain and limitations of the past into the joyful and unlimited world of Now. This book reveals in the simplest way how to still the mind and become fully present and awake in the truth of life.

As an essential part of his guidance into the present moment, the author penetrates deeply into the mystery of our existence. He reveals the hidden keys to enlightenment. He provides insight into the deepest questions which we must face if we are to become fundamentally free. He speaks of the soul's journey in a way that brings the whole of life into perspective and transforms problems and difficulties into opportunities for awakening.

Perhaps the most important aspect of this book is the author's unique insight into the nature of the mind and ego. He describes in detail how the ego's resistance to Presence is the primary obstacle to awakening and how we can overcome that resistance in a simple and effective way.

Each page of this book reveals a part of the mystery. There are hidden keys to awakening on every page. It is like a road map home.

To order a copy of Journey into Now,
Visit www.leonardjacobson.com

OTHER BOOKS BY LEONARD JACOBSON

In Search of the Light
A children's picture book for children and adults
Illustrated by Fiammetta Dogi,
Florence, Italy
ISBN No 978-1-890580-05-6

Spiritual teacher, Leonard Jacobson shares some of the secrets to finding inner joy and happiness in this beautifully illustrated story which helps children overcome fear and judgment and find that quiet inner place of peace and silence.

Come on a journey of discovery with Ned the Horse, Peter Rabbit, Bert the brave little Bumblebee and Molly Mouse as they set off in search of the light. Guided by the wind, our reluctant heroes pass through the forest of fear, eventually finding their way to a land where nothing seems right.

Following instructions given to them by several wise characters they meet along the way, they discover a path which leads them straight to the source of the light. When they find what they are searching for, they are so amazed that they laugh and dance with joy and delight.

To order a copy of In Search of the Light,
Visit www.leonardjacobson.com

LIBERATING JESUS, THE MOVIE

Liberating Jesus is a film of the remarkable one-man play, written and performed by Leonard Jacobson. Leonard plays the role of Jesus returned.

In 1981, Leonard experienced the first of a series of profound, spontaneous spiritual awakenings, in which he received some startling revelations about Jesus. Although these revelations affirmed the divinity of Jesus at the deepest level, nevertheless there were some astounding departures from traditional Christian beliefs.

The time is now. Jesus has returned after a long and difficult journey since his death upon the cross. He has much to share with us about his life and death, and how his teaching has been misunderstood and misused. The returned Jesus shows us a way out of separation and conflict and reveals the Oneness at the very heart of all paths and traditions. This film will either inspire, enlighten and delight you, or it will disturb you. It is very powerful. Feeling overwhelmed by what was revealed, Leonard chose not to speak of this for many years, until in 2006 he wrote the play, Liberating Jesus and performed it live in Los Angeles and Santa Cruz, California. He also performed the play at the Unity Village in Kansas before an audience of over five hundred people, many of whom were members of the clergy.

If you would like to watch the movie, *Liberating Jesus,* please visit www.leonardjacobson.com/liberatingjesus

A word of caution: If you are a Christian who adheres to traditional Christian beliefs, rituals and practices, you probably should not watch this movie. Leonard has no intention or desire to offend anyone.

Comments from those who saw the play or watched the movie.

"This story is so powerful. I can feel its deep truth resonating in me. Everyone with ears to hear needs to experience this hidden treasure." H.S., France

"I have prayed for a film such as this that tells the truth about Jesus. Such a courageous and bold film and yet it is needed right now more than ever!" R.B., United Kingdom

"True teaching is an art. It comes from one who has lived and embodied and integrated the experience being taught. Leonard, your offering of Liberating Jesus is so authentic. Your journey to Presence, wholeness and an embodied Christ Consciousness is so moving. Your voice is a beacon and a blessing." M.A., USA

"Liberating Jesus is a poignant, authentic, one-man original play loaded with simple, meaningful, powerful and clear contemporary explanations of Jesus' teachings. M.W., Colorado, USA

"All I can say is WOW. I saw Leonard perform this in Provence and was speechless after it. I have just watched it again and I am speechless again. Thank you so much for sharing it." H.M, Ireland

"A big note of THANKS for sharing your film and your message. So beautifully written and presented. I am very grateful for this message which is so timely in our world." D.N., Oregon, USA

"I recently had the opportunity of watching Liberating Jesus and absolutely loved it. Thank you so much for your Presence and all that you are." R.P, Canada

Comments from those who saw the play or watched the movie.

"I just watched Liberating Jesus and resonated very deeply with the intention and content. As a spiritual seeker, my path has embraced different wisdom traditions and an immersion in Biblical teachings has been my primary frame of reference. The difficulty that I faced was the contradiction between the voice of my heart and the predominant church representation of the meaning of scripture. After years of de-programming Christian belief systems, my conclusions are the same as yours. Thank you for your courage in stepping forward to guide others into conscious awakening." M.H., USA

"Hello Leonard, I was really happy to receive your announcement of Liberating Jesus and I passed it on to our minister at our local church. He is a former Catholic priest from Ireland and was so excited about the play that this past Sunday, for the zoom church service, he played the entire video. It blew people away. Again, Leonard, we deeply appreciate the Presence and guidance you provide to so many on the journey of awakening. We bless you and send you our good wishes for health and safety." D.K., USA

"I just watched *Liberating Jesus.* I love the simple clarity of Leonard's message. I'm so very grateful to have found this source of clear and beautiful wisdom." R.P., USA

"Thank you for your offering of Liberating Jesus. Such a perfect time to watch, listen and be absorbed in the pure Truth. You spoke directly to my heart and soul. I feel rightly renewed and resolved to keep my attention focused on the present moment." L.B., USA

Comments from those who saw the play or watched the movie.

"Thank you for the opportunity to watch Liberating Jesus. I watched it yesterday. I am an Eastern Orthodox Christian and I realize that the film contains serious elements that are foreign to the basis of our faith, which I am choosing to overlook.

I found in this film an enlightening description of a basic aspect of the true Christian life; something that is consistent with the nature of our inner work on the Christian Orthodox path. This particular element of the film has had a very positive impact on me, acting as an inspiration and further encouragement in bringing more awareness of what I am doing in living the Christian life, and I am thankful for this.

As a film, I found it to be especially well presented: the music, the photography, the "acting", the whole organization of it. There is a strong vibration of earnestness in what is presented, both in the elements I do not want to discuss and in the elements that I found useful and inspiring for my spiritual work." R.V., Greece